closure

mada plummer

closure

… where hope and struggle intersect …

mada plummer

Closure

Collection of Poetry and Lagniappe
Copyright © 2006 by Mada Plummer

Published by:
Merging Minds
PO Box 1911
Pflugerville TX 78691

ISBN # 978-0-6151-3845-9   Softcover

Acknowledgments

"How Did She," **From a Bend in the River: 100 New Orleans Poets**, Runagate Press, 1998; "me auntie lou," **Singularities: Writing from the Center of the Edge**, 2001

Photographs by mada plummer unless otherwise noted

This book was printed in the United States of America.

Dedication

To Mom and Dad, and Generations of women bent but not broken, we honor your lives by remembering your words and imitating your examples of love. "Thank You."

To My sons, Ian and Silas, and my grandchildren, Shamyra, Shanice and Silas, Jr., you have been entrusted with our family's legacy, cherish it.

To My friend and author Julie Smith, for being touched by the words that honored my mother. "Thank You"

To a unique circle of individuals, Dr. M. Markley, Dr. M. Kimbrough, Steve Vera, Debra M., Jésus L., Lorenza S., Earnest Lee D., Irma Jean J., Element615, M. Bentley, my fellow 935rs and all who kept pushing. "Thank You" for your smiles and encouragement.

"Do not be anxious over anything, but in everything by prayer and supplication along with thanksgiving let our petition be made known to God: and the peace of God that excels all thought will guard your hearts and your mental powers by means of Christ Jesus."

—Philippians 4:6, 7

Foreword

In a court of law, a jury of twelve peers decides a man's fate or his *closure*.

In a different court of law, a jury of twelve words determines mine.

Forgive us our trespasses,

As we forgive those who trespass against us ...

Table of Contents

healing

a place less-traveled to rearrange thoughts

Rite of Passage

Today, we celebrate

Your inauguration into womanhood.

In this rite of passage,

We pass on to you

What was passed on to us.

In you

Are colors of many generations;

With you

Are words powerful as thunderstorms.

Words that

Strike like lightning

Roar like thunder and

Cleanse like rain.

Our Girl-child

As you cross this threshold,

The tools with you since birth

Will guide you

As you embrace life. And

Before we

Fall as snow falls

To the pavement and

Die, we

Leave with you,

Life Words that

Were left with us.

Speak softly: You'll be heard.
For the value of yours words
Lies not in volume
But in essence.
Be aware of your surroundings and
Those who fill them. Learn from both.
Be patient with your questions in the evening for
The answers are on the horizon in the morning.
Praise Jah
That your journey over grass is not complicated;
Take note of Him
That your life may blossom in peace;
Be true to yourself and to others.
Our Girl-child,
In you
Are features of
Many generations:
Eyes, wide as saucers,
Shine like polished diamonds;
Eyebrows, smooth as velvet,
Bend like limbs of a leafless tree;
Hips, strong as armor, carry the next generation.
So lift your head and
Walk in the richness of autumn's wealth,
Be comfortable with summer in your complexion.
Our Girl-child,
The time will come
When the other half of your equation
Will appear and

Grow into your life.

His caress

Will cause you to

Sway like a weeping willow on its knees;

He will lovingly lead you to

Move smoothly in the high silence of pleasure

And be so devoted to you,

He will catch your smile before it

Hits the ground; he will

Gaze into your hot brown eyes, and

Enjoy the feel of your skin that

Shines like the dew of fever.

He will welcome you to

Curl into the comfort of his arms and

Enhance all sweetness in you.

He will not cause your eyes to curve

Into shameful sickles or

Be encircled by dark crescents or

Abuse you and transform your bronze skin to ash.

He will not fracture your spirit

With defeating words or

Disrespect you

With shameful acts or

Elevate himself by putting you down.

When the other half of your equation

Comes home from work with his face

Covered with sweat; when he

Beats the rim of his hat against his leg,

Pushes open the door and

Makes its hinges weep,
You know
That he knows
That he
Comes to his heaven
Where you, *Our girl-child*,
The other half of *his* equation
Will reward him with
The miracle of your smile,
The coziness of your arms, and be set free in
The sanctuary of your bosom.
Hold on to the positive things
You say to each other in the pocket of night;
Use each other to grow and
To grow on;
Fill each other with the intimacy
You crave *from* each other; and
As you walk beneath trees
That group themselves as a community,
Meditate on the history of
How whole families
Bent their backs in fields and
Surrendered their burdens to
Wade in the ecstasy of river baptism.
The time *will* come
When your newborn will
Search for the taste of your nipples and
Be filled with its sweet water;
The time *will* come

When your breasts will
Dry up and droop in your night gown;
Silver strands will
Cover your head like a hat and
Give power and authority to your face;
Be glad, wear these as evidence
That you have fulfilled your purpose.
Our Girl-child,
Be free
Of what holds you back,
Avoid those 'crabs in the barrel'
Who because of failed dreams and
Dark hearts,
Feed on negative thinking that
Resonates so deeply,
They want company,
Your company to
Merge with their misery.
In this rite of passage,
We pass on to you
What was passed on to us.
So before the light in your eyes
Dims; or
The strength in your legs
Fades; or
The blood that
Flows freely through your cistern
Dries;

When it is time,

You

Shall celebrate

Your daughter's

Inauguration into womanhood

Because

In you

Are colors of many generations;

With you

Are powerful words that

Strike

Roar and

Cleanse

Like

Lightning

Thunder and

Rain.

Beyond the Ashes

While staring at the orange glow of a dying fire,
I feed on memories that roam through me
The way the sun's shadow
Dances through the forest.
A memory of how we used to
Run through soft dust storms of powdered earth
Created by my brothers' feet
As they kicked dirt to the sky.

How we wiped our school uniforms
With fingers stained
With drippings from fresh mulberries that
Melted sweetly on our tongues. We
Inhaled the fragrance of thick, syrupy sap that
Clung to our clothes and stuck to our hands as
We climbed the pine tree in our front yard;

From the highest limb,

We sat and overlooked the canal below,

From where a snapper turtle crawled and

Where crawfish

Hid among full-grown cat-tails. We

Anchored ourselves in a place that was

Heaven-high to us

For a glimpse of the

Earthen levee that separated us

From the mighty Mississippi.

A memory of our bare toes that curled and uncurled then

Grabbed bunches of thick clovers

Dressed in avocado green

Topped with tiny scented white flowers

On which bumble bees dined. We

Sneaked into our grandpa's melon patch, pried open

Ripe cantaloupe and watermelon once

Shielded beneath wide lettuce-colored leaves and

Sampled the first fruits of his harvest;

With straw hats on our heads that provided shade on our necks,

And long-sleeved shirts that defended

Our tender skin from the summer sun, while

Bent on one knee, we ooched,

Dragged, and filled wooden bushels

For three bits' wages so

Grandpa's harvest could be picked

And sold at the French Market

At the foot of Decatur Street

And the River.

As a reward, we stood in a long line

At Café du Monde for a bag of hot beignets

Covered by a cloud of fine powdered sugar and

A cup of café au lait.

With curious eyes, we stared at tourists

Possessed by lusting palates in search of

Culinary ecstasy to fulfill their addictions.

Mules in straw hats were

Hitched to open-aired buggies

As their rhythmic hoofs

Drummed loudly on old brick streets

En route to the paint-peeling gates of Jackson Square

Pass Creole cottages off Ursuline and St. Philip Streets and

One of the best kept sweet secrets, Croissant D'Or.

We chased and inhaled

The soft perfume of Calla Lilies on which

Birds and bees dined and buzzed in unrehearsed dances.

These images

Relight my head with what family is.

While staring at the orange glow of a dying fire,

Calm passed through me

Like a fallen feather

From a stiff-winged brown pelican that

Floated down the Mississippi;

Within the heart of this calm, more

Familial memories lined up to be

Refreshed, reheated and retold.

Fondly, I recall how beads of kitchen sweat

Trickled in a crooked path toward the valley of

Grandma's bosom

As she stirred a hearty pot of stew to feed her brood;

I remember the nighttime quiet of our house where

The music of whistling winds were loud as thunder

Where the aroma of approaching rain

Lured us to retreat to bed and

Hide from the world in undisturbed sleep.

The orange glow of a dying fire

Has yielded to gray ash and

Calm has been stifled *again*

By a twenty-five year old memory

Folded like a handkerchief;

In one of its creases

Was the face of a creature who

Changed the temperature of my blood;

Who made me tough instead of brave when he

Forced his seed into my soil,

Poisoned my thighs,

Subtracted joy from my life and

Dirtied me so badly,

I didn't like myself.

His seed sprouted, but

Died inside of me early one morning and

Dangled as if

Disconnected from the cord of life.

On an ER gurney, in the corner

Away from

Eyes and ears of other ailing and wailing patients,

Clumps of thick tissue,

The color of grape jelly,

Were extracted

From the deepest part of me.

I laid numb

As if absent from my own body.

In the afterbirth of a dying fire,

This part of my past

Still has a lien on

Parts of my present.

Twenty-five years later,

I sometimes still feel

Trapped in someone else's breath.

Someday,

Beyond the ashes

I will walk

With a friend, and be

No longer afraid

To talk about dark,

Hurtful things

I could not name.

Closure

Yesterday, I was
A tired soul with empty eyes and
Wanted to just
Walk off the edge of the universe
As my brain burned with
Defeating thoughts
That echoed for decades. I needed to be
Calmed by the dark while I
Searched the definition of life.
Yesterday, I didn't understand
Why would a man who
Promised to love,
Honor and
Cherish *allegedly*
Point a loaded double-barrel shotgun at me
And our unborn child
As I offered
Silent undressed prayers?
Why would a man who
Promised to love,
Honor and
Cherish but
Driven to hurt me
As much as he hated himself *allegedly*
Ram a six inch dull blue candle so deep inside of me
It nearly punctured my womb?

Ashamed and afraid, I told no one,

Not even my mother - the sister of my heart.

Why would a man who

Promised to love,

Honor and

Cherish *allegedly*

Sacrifice my freedom to

Market bags of addiction

Then stalked and harassed me for

Reclaiming my life?

Today,

I have made peace

With my past and

Gone are nights when I'd awaken,

Gasping for air as

A herd of nightmares

Too vivid to forget, choked me.

Nightmares that

Squeezed incomprehensible sounds and

Incoherent whispers from my throat

As my heart hammered

My chest.

Gone are days when I'd sit

Staring at the sky

Until my eyes burned

Without blinking. I realize -

Regret is a waste of time and

Dare not count how much time I

Have wasted.

I have made peace

With a past that goes

Everywhere I go;

One

That hummed and hissed

Like a dying fluorescent light;

One

Where tears formed

A river in my bosom whenever I

Drew from the deep well of fond memories of

My mother and father

Whose ashes

Have long ago

Mingled with the earth

And whose bleached bones

Have been washed

By ancient rivers but

The rhythmic roar of their words

Have hung around.

I dusted off my

Deferred dreams

And now move

Passionately toward them. I am not

Mournful that the puzzle of life

Still has missing pieces but enjoy little things like

Watching the Sun

Being swallowed by a Gulf horizon;

Sitting under a tin roof

During a heavy rain;

Being lulled by the noisy patter of raindrops;
Admiring rainbow hues
Too delicate to hold the eyes and
Whose seams bleed and blend into each other.
Today,
I am free
From the margins of those who
Stood next to me,
Looked into my eyes, and said, "I do."
I am free
From their gangrenous messages.
Though many knotted experiences
Remain yet to untie and
Much underbrush to clear away,
I accept that I cannot
Erase events from my heart or
Edit scenes from my head
Of a history uncut or
Ignore the empty spaces of
Unfulfilled years
Outlined by dust.
But at least
I am done
Drowning in
Bad memories
Of poor choices.

Today,

I eat

The fruit of closure and

Fill my lungs

With the peace

That morning brings.

Photographer unknown

Smells of Home

In the soft evening air as
A whisper of sun remains,
From behind missing windows that resemble black eyes,
Damp footprints on my grandma's front porch
Resurrect smells of home.

They overtake me like a raging river
That stampedes everything in its path.
Mmm, the smells of home,
Yeast for light breast rising under a clean dish rag
In a dark corner on the kitchen counter;
Fresh figs and pears bubbling and boiling in separate pots as
We wait with anxious tongues to

Lick the spoon that stirred winter's preserves.

The air in grandma's kitchen

Was sharp with the aroma of home-made soup

Eaten on rainy days and cold nights; and

Sweet potato pies

Spiced with cinnamon, nutmeg and vanilla extract.

Now and then, her kitchen was

Overpowered by the odor of burnt rice.

These memorable smells

Snap like clean bed sheets and pillowcases

Drying on back yard clotheslines.

From behind missing windows that resemble black eyes,

I saw my shoulders

Squeezed between grandma's knees

As I sat on a stack of Sears catalogs,

Destined for the outhouse,

With each pull of the comb, she

Separated my hair like

Plowed rows of corn and purple hull peas,

Then rubbed a fingertip's worth of Royal Crown

On my scalp until it shined like skin at midnight.

Regrettably, I wish I hadn't napped as she

Passed on memories of her life as part of my inheritance.

Now, bits and pieces of a generation of women who

Were the toughest links in our growing chain

Are getting lost along with

Images of their chocolate eyes, warm as fire,

Skin, coffee-colored and caramel smooth that blushed in the sun,

Hair, coal black and long enough to

Fall behind their shoulders and

Hang like silk scarves;

A generation of women

Whose hearts beat hard as

Thunder;

Whose stories

Struck us the way lightning stabbed the sky.

From behind missing windows that resemble black eyes

In the soft evening air,

Rooms in grandma's house

Are empty

And the river of brothers, sisters and their children

Is drying up.

These days children seldom

Walk in their grandpa's big shoes

Or tilt their heads to the sky and name clouds

Or soothe their skins in a light drizzle,

Or wrap themselves in grandma's shawl.
These days, empty wine bottles and beer cans
Sleep on their sides in fields
Where corn, melon and okra were
Grown to feed the family.
I saw sweat pour like rain from the necks of kinfolk
Who fed on acid instead of apples
Crack instead of corn flakes
Heroin instead of ham hocks
Meth instead of melons.
I hold my head down
Not out of shame, but
Disappointed that dusty air,
Filled the same room
Where grandma used to
Spread thick quilts
Made from hand-me-downs,
A room where we laid as
Thunder announced rain and
Clouds puffed up like purple-stained pillows
And where the strong scent of rain
Rode in on the warm air then
Drifted through open doors and windows;
We did not see the rain as we
Fell into hypnotic sleep as grandma
Sat in her rocking chair and
Watched over us
As if we were treasure-
And we were.

In the soft evening air,

From behind missing windows that resemble black eyes

In these rooms, womenfolk

Who suffered

More than their share of history,

Gathered and passed on

How not to damage the property

In our heads and

Between our legs; and

How not to put our secret flesh on public display.

These days, the smells of home

We left behind and

The ones we return to

Have scattered

Like dandelion wish-weed.

Eyes of the Have-nots

Eyes bright as two pale moons
Filled with history
Cry every night for you.
Eyes that cut through years
And saw schools torched
With bottled cocktails;
Front yards scorched
With burnt crosses;
Grown men beaten like children
Children whipped like men
Women, who wore vacant expressions,
As if not connected to their own bodies
While being raped and who were
Threatened not to
Let go of long, echoes or screams;
Necks of young men,
Snapped like dry twigs,
Dangled like broken tree limbs.
Dignity stripped away
At someone else's discretion.
Eyes
Soft as the underneath of a dove's wing
Saw ribbons of smoke
Rise from a blacksmith's fire that crafted
Branding irons

Heated until red as blood then

Tattooed into toast brown skin.

Eyes

Of a grandmother

With hair the color of moth's wings, who

Clawed at her own throat

Until beads of red painted her breasts;

Her eyes

Swollen with tears that

Marched down her cheeks and

Congregated under her chin

Because the girl-child of her girl-child

Was ripped from her –

Not like unborn eyes that

Disappeared in a cloud of strawberry red,

But in PMSing waters that

Broke bloated levees and marked the land

Like a heavy menstrual flow.

Eyes that

Returned to a home forever

Changed where once-grand magnolias

Stood along Elysian Fields like proud southern women

Now dress like cypress trees in Henderson Swamp.

Eyes

Full of despair that were ignored by leaders who

Played *eeny, meeny, miney, moe* with their lives.

"Have-nots" who no longer "Get Not" because they

"Fit Not" into the new scheme that "Will Not" foster the plan to

Rebuild a drowned city with better levees and smarter leaders.

Eyes that belong to a people not knowing where to

Replant their roots that beg to be part of the land;

"Have-nots" who have no say in the blueprints to

Reestablish their neighborhoods that are

Now absent traces of the past, present and possibly the future;

Reworked strategies exclude the initiative to

Reunite families or

Return a culture

To its rightful place.

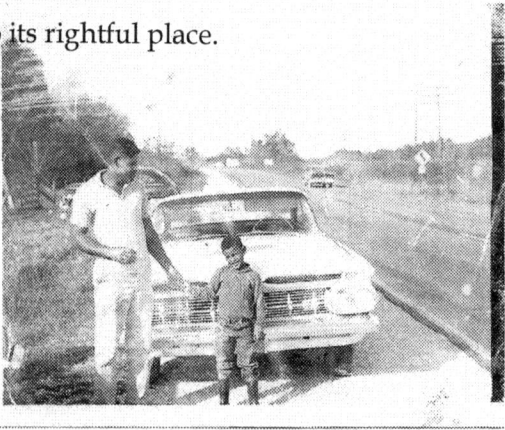

Highway 23 South, Nairin, Louisiana - Photographer unknown

If only these

Eyes can

Re-write

The script receding waters

Left behind and

Re-draw deep footprints

Erased

From my birthplace.

living

Before no one's left

We gotta do something
Before no one's left
To remember what family is or
Where the memory of family lives
Because these days
It seems we only get together
When there's a cold, well-dressed,
Made-up body
To put away in a grave
Under a granite stone or a crude
Painted wooden cross
With three lines
That fails to tell their whole story.
Lines that bear very little history:
A name,
When you came into the world,
When you left, and sometimes *how* you left.
But that's not how it should be
And we gotta do something
Before no one's left
To welcome each other with the warmth of mighty hugs or
Plant lingering wet kisses
On unfamiliar family cheeks or
Hear an auntie with a wide smile say,

"Come on in.

I was thankin' 'bout y'all this mornin'," or

Listen under an open window as Big Mama

Hummed, *Gimme that ol' time religion,* a time when we

Playfully chased her biddies and geese and

Sat on her screened porch as walls of evening fog

Shut out the sun; and where

In a deafening silence, the song of mosquitoes

Searching for hot blood

Became an audible whine as we

Watched bright red taillights

Fade into nights blue as Indian ink; or

Played under the shadow of the large oak tree in her back yard or

Swung from its monstrous branches or

Soared as high as her tin roof.

Now, that's how it used be

And we still gotta do something

Before no one's left

To sit at the kitchen table

When the house is

Nighttime quiet to reflect on blessings; and

Before the rooster screams,

Rise before the sun and

Walk as far as the soles of our feet take us to

Look over our inheritance, and

Be determined to preserve

And not sell for 30 pieces of silver or swap for insatiable addictions

What our parents' parents' parents' parents'

Bought and paid with their blood and sweat and

What was held as our inheritance.

That's how it should to be

And we gotta do something

Before no one's left who will

Drive hundreds of miles

From south to central Louisiana

So that granddaughters and grandsons can

Sit and bounce on the laps of

Grandmas and grandpas and to

Listen as their rocking chairs weep while they

Fill the air with stories of days which

These descendants

May never experience - like

Walking barefoot or in broken shoes for five miles

To a one-room schoolhouse to "learn your lesson"

Which was no more than

readin', *ritin'* and *'rithmetic* or

Going no further than the sixth grade for boys or

Eighth grade for girls

Because you had to give up schooling to

Work the farm

Before the sun came up, and

Long after it went down;

Or sneak to read the Bible while

Sitting in the shadow

Of the low light of a kerosene lamp or

Chop wood to

Feed the pot-bellied stove or

Heat pots of water to fill a

Galvanized tub for bathing

'Cause there ain't no indoor bathroom; or

Sleep under quilts

Made from hand-me-downs that

Couldn't go around anymore.

That's how it used to be

And we gotta do something

Before no one's left

We had no telephones,

Cell phones, faxes, E-mail, Blackberries but
We had pen, paper and three-cent stamps; and we
Took the time to write letters that
All started with
Just a few lines to let you know …
Mothers and fathers loaded their children
Into the family car on Sundays then drove nineteen miles or more
To share a meal, cut a yard, or visit the sick in order to
Maintain the bonds of family;
There was a time
When grown folk and children sat
Together in *one* room and
Watched *one* black and white television
And passed on a tradition of villagedom.
That's how it used to be -
That's how it needs to be
And we gotta do something
Before
Our bones return to the shelf
And no one's left.

How Did She

There were six of us at the dinner table

With enough food to feed only three.

After giving thanks,

We all got our fill

And sometimes, there was enough

To feed a neighbor's hungry child.

How did she?

How did she

Manage to take the little money

My daddy made at the shipyard

-$1.58 an hour, 72 hours a week-

And stretch it to the four corners of the earth

To make sure there was a roof over our heads,

Enough to buy plaid fabric to make shirts for the twins,

Drapes for the windows

And now and then, a dress for my colored baby doll?

How did she?

How did she

Wangdoogle our being the first family in our neighborhood

To have an indoor toilet – no, a full indoor bathroom

Which meant no more long walks down that beaten path

To that wooden door that half-hung on hinges

Kept closed by a bent nail on the outside

And a screen door fastener on the inside

So we could have the luxury of taking a bath

In that round galvanized tub?

How did she?
How did she
Have enough love to go around
So that none of us felt left out?
She didn't give to one without giving to the other or
To cousins who came over
Because their mothers were busy washing clothes
Others not her own would wear or
Cooking food for the mouths of another's brood;
We shot marbles, spun top
Climbed the pine tree in our front yard
Crawled under the house,
Watched grown-ups walk by,
Laid on our backs on the front "garry" and
Named shapes of clouds that moved slowly across the sky-
And some of them resembled
Spilled milk,
How did she?
How did she
Keep a happy heart in hard times?
How did she?
It's a thing called
Mother's love.

A Mother's Heartache

Theresa's mother sat silently
The way snow fell and laid quietly.
In midnight darkness, she
Recalled the essence of a daughter now
Hidden in earth's womb and safe in God's memory.
A mother's eyes
Drained of what eyes were made for -
To see her daughter run on ballerina toes
Towards the comfort of her bosom.
Theresa's mother knew and did not accept
That her daughter would not
Cross into womanhood
Or march up the aisle to say, "I do"
Or experience the pangs of labor and the joys of birthing
Or her first kiss
Or paint her lips wicked red.
Some days the light in her eyes
Appeared burned out as
She sat like a bird on an electric wire.
Other days, she rocked as if waiting
For morning to come
With a different script as
She held onto Theresa's sweater or
Anything absorbed with her history.
Sometimes she listened in vain
For her daughter's voice and

Laughter that was strong as the sound of waterfalls.

April, 1957, a red Cadillac

Fatally struck her firstborn. Her tiny body

Hurled 20 feet towards heaven as she watched her baby

Fall to the highway like a shot put.

For a while, Theresa's mother closed her eyes and avoided

Purple morning sunrises and

Turned her back to the calm of

Warm honey sunsets;

Highway 23 South, Sunrise, Louisiana - Photographer unknown

She withdrew to a place where memories could

Crawl across her mind like a herd of summer clouds

So that she could cry uninterrupted

In a quiet place to help ease

Sorrow that engulfed her head,

Sadness that consumed her heart, and

Tears that poured from her eyes

Like a thunderstorm.

Embroidered stories

Did little to change the temperature of her blood

Or fill her empty arms

Or incite her to find new dreams

To replace old ones.

If the ocean had heaved and

Sent forth

Its rhythms to soothe her pain,

She'd only sink in the smells of her daughter

And rock back and forth as if lost.

A mother who watched a world of living things

Dribble away as

She started each day with unrested hands

That could not beat back the pangs of that

Life-changing day.

In the morning, she trembled

Like a newly baptized child;

In the evening, she refused to travel

Emotional distances to a river of relatives

To help quench the absence that

Surrounded her like a dry sack.

This is the anguish of a mother

With a crushed heart.

Theresa's mother knew and did not accept

That her daughter would not

Cross into womanhood

Or march up the aisle to say, "I do"

Or experience the pangs of labor and the joys of birthing

Or her first kiss

Or paint her lips wicked red.
Thirty-two years after the earth was zipped and
Her daughter was hidden away like treasure,
Theresa's mother and father
Both entered into a well-deserved rest. Left behind,
We have inherited the awful emptiness of
Our mother's eyes; and memories of
Our father's long face stained with
Tears shed on birthdays, holidays and anniversaries.
Our faces don't reflect the sun much;
We endure a place inside of us
That they suffered.
One we did not know existed until now and
Understand better the depth of their pain
That burned like an eternal flame;
One, the wind
Could not blow out.
We each try to hold onto
Evidences that bind us together
And attempt to put words around
A pain that can never be
Explained.

Dear God

I never understood why mama
Laid across the bed
With my brothers and me during naptime
And cried. As I browsed through her book
Of sweet sad memories 35 years later and found out why.
Story pictures of how my sister
Used to brush my daddy's hair and
How he eventually went bald where
You could spot him in a corn field
On a breezy afternoon;
Of how she
Dropped one of the twins in the toilet,
Because she wanted to help mama potty train them;
Of how she
Cupped her left hand around mama's chin
And stared into her soul.
I tell my son of how mama
Waited at the bottom of the pine tree
In our front yard until I climbed down
So she could make me
Put on that pale yellow dress
With white lace, gathered at the waist,
A big bow tied to the back
And three layers of can-can underneath
That made me look like a church bell when I walked;
Of how she
Chased me from under the bed

With a hook-nosed broom
Worn from sweeping dirt from corners,
So she could spank me for painting
My face with her red lipstick;
Of how she
Parted and braided my hair
Into three ponytails the way I liked it.
Four years after my parents' deaths,
I laid across my son's bed during his naptime
And cried. He asked,
"Mommy, are you sad about your mom and dad?"
"Yes." And with all that he had,
He stretched his arms around me and
In his innocence offered old-soul comfort,
"Come on, sugar. You'll see them again.
Let me make you feel better," then he sang
Amazing grace, how sweet the sound, he
Stopped and prodded,
"Come on, mommy, you have to sing if you want to feel better."
And as if
Touched by his grandparents' spirits
And the spirits of those he did not know, he whispered,
"You can think of me as your mom and dad."
In a flood of tears, I asked,
"If you were my mom and dad, what would you say to me?"
"I would say, *I love you*."

Gracie

In things that frame the basic story of life,

We think of you,

Watching a sunset through a yellow haze

Walking in your back yard before morning dew evaporates

Listening to the steady tap of rain on the window

Sitting at the table drinking strong coffee

Smiling at your children as they tossed fresh cut grass;

Wiping playground sweat from their foreheads

Crossing the street to shake hands with a neighbor

Gathering at Sunday dinner to

Share memories like washing on washboards, taking baths

With homemade lye soap; covering up with handmade quilts,

Drinking red Kool-Aid from a Mason jar.

It's in these things that frame the basic story of life,

We think of you, Aunt Gracie.

Though this hour of sorrow

Feels like forever in all directions, there is a blessing.

You pulled us from around the world

To celebrate life-yours, ours and how they intertwine;

You pulled us from around the world

To remind us of what not to take for granted.

Though our hearts are heavy, and

Sorrow roars through us like

A freight train through a thunderstorm,

It's in the things that frame the basic story of life,

We think of you.

We honor you and the chapters of your life and

This is the time for us to read aloud the stories

You wrote during your lifetime and left with us.

In this hour that feels like forever, there is a blessing.

Before ten o'clock on September 4, 2004,

Though there was no strength in your body

To breathe on your own or

To raise your hand to wave goodbye or

To fix a smile or

To whisper, *I'm almost home, now,*

While surrounded by family,

You opened your eyes one last time and

After one last look –

Like headlights in thick morning fog -

They disappeared

As the curtains to the windows of your soul

Closed slowly.

We rejoiced as you drifted

Photographer unknown

"To walk in the light,
The Beautiful light
Somewhere the dew drops of mercy shine bright
Shine all around us by day and by night"
There were 70 chapters
To your book of life as
You signed your name on the last line
With your last breath and

It's in these things that frame the basic story of life

We remember you.

Madear

The wrinkles that landscape your face don't reveal
The history in your soft eyes that still
Crinkle at the corner whenever you smile.
Eyes that used to follow us everywhere we went,
Whether playing with baby dolls made from Coke bottles,
Or leaving a cloud of dust when we rode stick horses;
Or playing hopscotch in your driveway
Or pulling a barge made from a block of wood and a
Piece of string in a swollen ditch after a heavy rain.
As we sift through a lifetime of memories, sadly, no longer
Does the aroma of the outdoors follow you into your kitchen;
Gone are days when family members who traveled
Long distances would pull into your driveway
For a country breakfast and a heaping of familiness.
Though some memories have scattered like ash in the wind,
Thoughts of you will always produce new sunsets in us and
Your rocking chair stories still bring to life what our family is.
Sometimes when we look into your eyes
They are distant and dreamy
Other times, there is a curious twinkle of familiarity as
A community of recollections dance in your head as you wring
Your soft hands that tell where hope and struggle long ago met.
So before any more time passes, we thank you and
Honor you, Madear, because you did your part to
Shape the land that mothered us and to
Change a river that watered us.

Me Auntie Lou

There she go that jumaica woman
Hey, dat be me auntie lou, and she be like a cat,
Always landin' on her feet.
One summa, me walk tru her livin' room
And on di dey wall she sho me
In gold picture frames, side-by-side
Husbands numbers 5, 6 and 7.
Me tinkin' dose her gray-hair brothas.
She be tellin' me "Come chil, let me tell ya 'bout these men."
Husband number 5, *He* was a good man
He bought me dis house and ev'rytin' in it;
Husband number 6, *He* was a good man
He make sure I haf sometin' nice to ride in,
He be tellin' me, "Don't charge no batt'ry, buy a new one."
She be tinkin' that 'bout husbands.
Husband number 7, *He* was a very good man,
He sho me the world, and
Made me heart beat harder than young fellas.
So far, auntie lou, me go pass husband number tree
"Why you marry that turd mon anyway?"
Me not quite sure.
"Oh, po chil, let me tell you sometin',
You don't go marry no mon because you luv him,
You marry him because him got money.
Me can't go to LP&L Electric Company

And tell the mon, "me can't pay me bill
But me got a mon and him luv me good."
What you tink they tell me?
Auntie, sometimes me cousins be teasin'
"Ya know tree strikes you out, gurl."
Me tell dem, "You don't know baseball,
It takes nine strikes to get the team out.
Me got six more swings."
Me auntie lou,
Well, she was no gold digga
She was a bizness woman!

To Mi Auntie Lou

Mi a go tell yuh be lik mi madda
Be proud, 'cause mi find Peace dat
Flo' 'tru mi di like di words of Bob Marley
Dance in Jam-Down breeze,
Reaching up dem green hills of Mo Bay
And all di way to di river that fall in Ochee.
Mi a go marry no mo not 'cause mi cousin, he tell me,
"Gurl, yuh be having mo husband dan mi got fingas
On mi left hand."
Mi I tell im, "Mi still got mi thumb."
Mi fin'ly lern Auntie Lou, 'sum'tin 'bout men,
Dis not a matta of what im got
But what im is and what im do wit what im have.

Louisiana Girl

As soon as I cross the Sabine,

Bienvenue la Louisiane

A Louisiana mist races in with this greeting

From Bayou LeBoeuf and other serpentine bayous

And Henderson Swamp

Where cypress trees stand like legions of the dead.

As soon as I cross the Sabine,

Obsidian black nights hide my face less the story of my life.

As I drive through the cycle of night to reach

The rhythm of a land

Where in graveyard quiet,

Ancestral sermons

Rise from the earth; I struggle to stay awake to

Listen to dialogues between

Humans and rivers, ravens and stars.

I savor the recipe in songs

Heard as a child that

Fell away generations ago. Songs that

Reignite energies that move through me

As the sky yawns and as

The wind echoes across morning.

A history craves to know my eyes

As I cross the Sabine.

I sing because I'm happy. I sing because I am free.

His eyes are on the sparrow and I know He watches me.

Change Don' Come

Grabbin' hol'a her wawk'a,

Aunt Lauranne gits up reel slo' deez dayz

Frum her kitch'n table

Full'a nicks fer as long as I kin rememba, reckon dey git dere

From where folks mighta drop'a 'nife or a fawk,

Or maybe where one'a her chil'ren mighta

Press too hawd wit' pencils or ank pens wilz doin' dey lesson.

A tabul, wich is, uhm mo' den sho' is

Old'a den me and Daisee.

"Well, y'allz comp'ny is good,

Dats what de ol' folks use'ta say', so uhm gon' on in.

I see y'all in de morning,' if de Lawd say de sam."

Aunt Lauranne be makin' her way tru'

Her dinin' rum pass anutha tabul dat use'ta hol'

All kindz'a homemade two layer cakes and

Sweet potato and pumpkin pies

All 'rapped in ferl paper 'cept de

Coconut cake wit' a blood red cherry on top, and

De jelly cake made'a two layers of homemade goodness.

Aunt Lauranne make sho' Daisee cov'a dem wit'

Sum kleer plastik 'rap. Most'a daddy's auntees

Be no'in' dese his fav'rit, 'spechul'ly de banana cake.

Dat wuz a long time'a go win we use'ta come up here

Mo' reg'lar and wen Daisee use'ta have reel good dayz

Burnin' dem potz in de kitch'n, cookin' up a storm dat

Folks didn't mind eatin' and glad fer not hav'in'ta drive 19 milez

South to git sum'in ta eat in Bunkie.

My brotha Louis, aw'wa cudin' Irma Jean,

Daisee and me all sayz' "Amen" ta Aunt Lauranne as headz on in.

We lookz at her and Madear in'a spachul kinda way.

Reckon dats on account we all be'n touched

By sum'body close ta us dyin'. Reckon too 'cause deys

All we gotz lef' of'da old'a ginerashun.

De rum git reel quiet 'bout na.

Eyes stawtin' ta well up wit' wat'a. Dis here seem lik'a good time

Ta git my music box frum de nex' rum. I turnz it on and

Rat 'bout den Sam Cooke wuz playin'

"I wuz born by de riva, in a lil' tent

Oh jest lik' de riva, I been runnin' ever cents,

Itz been'a long, a long time comin'

But I 'no a change gon' come, oh yeez, it will,

Reckon if'n der wuz a dog in de yawd, he be bawkin' 'bout na.

Fo' as long as we be'n cumin' out'cheer,

I ain't never seent nun'a my cudins dance,

Pat dey feets, but never dance.

Itz be'n too hawd livin' and

Uhm'ma fraid ta die,

I don'no what's up der beyon' de sky,

Itz be'n a long, a long time comin'

But I 'no change gon' com, oh yeez it will ..."

Ob'lously, we wuzn't much on sangin' neetha.

Daisee stawts ta set de record scrate

"I don'no who you talkin' 'bout, but I kin sang."

Den Irma Jean tellz her, "I can hold a tune mysef

'Long as I stayz in de shaw'wa."

I ain't gon' lie, I can't sang, and ta put it lik' aw'wa Uncle Lucas

"I-I k-k-an't, s-s-s-sang b-b-but I-I-I kin, kin s-s-sho hum."

Na, don' fa'git 'bout aw'wa cudin Earnest Lee, na, h-h-he k-k-kin

Git'cha k-k-komin' and g-g-goin.'

Louis be teasin' Daisee, "well, na, if'n you don' mine,

We'ez all ears, gon' sang. Let us hear wha'cha got."

Daisee stawtz ta backin' out,

"Well, it ain't de sam. Uhm use'ta sangin' wit' a qu'aw'ya."

Fer sum reezin, wen'sa' never kin folk git tagetha

We all findz aw'wa self in de kitch'n.

'Long as we got sumin' ta chew on ev'n if it ain't no mo'

Den a slice'a bread and bolognie saw'ij,

Or potted meat and crackas,

Or ifn'n Daisee wantin' ta whip up sum

Scrabul eggs and rice, and we got sum'where ta sit,

We ain't goin' no where for a long time

And will stayz up till aw'wa eyes

Be crossin' accounta so sleepy. We hangz der 'cause it

Ain't oft'n we git ta be wit' fam'ly lik' dis.

Got sum strong coffee in fron'a us

Den we head on down mem'ry road.

Irma Jean stawts, "Memba wen

We use'ta git aw'wa hair comb'd wit'

A comb dat wuz one'a dem strange colorz dey don't

Ev'n make no mo'?"

Daisee remembaz too, "Yeah, and how dey use'ta dip

Dat comb in'a jar of Royal Crown den in sum wat'a.

Yeah, sur buddy,"

Reckon we wuz havin' sum sort'a serv'is up in here

'Cause we all be sayin' "Amen" ag'in.

Irma Jean keeps on, "Oh Lawd, do I rememba."

Daisee jumps in, "Yes, sur. It wudn't nuttin' nice.

It wuzn't so bad wen dey wuz partin' aw'wa hair,

It wuz win dey use'ta plait it."

We all leanz back and laf' reel hawd.

Y'all memba how aw'wa mama knuckles use'ta be diggin' in'

Aw'wa scalp makin' dips in aw'wa headz?"

Irma Jean rubz her head, "I kin still feel it. No matta wat,

I tell you one thang, I wud give anythang

Ta have mama plait my hair rat na."

Me too. Daisee be tryin' ta git aw'wa mind up,

Irma Jean sayz, "What 'bout how we use'ta sit on top'a de footstool

Or a stack'a catalogs 'tween aw'wa mama kneez

And ev'ry-time we fidgy, dey squeeze aw'wa shouldas,

I don' no "bout y'all but I wuz glad wen I lernt how'ta

Comb my own hair."

Daisee is on'a roll na, and she be reely wretchin' back,

"What 'bout wen we had'ta git aw'wa hair scraten',

Memba gittin' yo ears burnt?"

We shake aw'wa headz and laf reel hawd.

I memba wen mama use'ta scrate'n my hair on a sad'day night,

And dem she make me put'a pair of a drawz on my head

Sos it didn' git mess'd up wilez I slept.

I nos I ain't de only one up in here who had'ta do that neetha.

Irma Jean menchun, "How 'bout dem pink foam curlas?"

We all lookz at Daisee 'cause she still be wearin'

Foam curlas deez days, ;ceptin' dey is yello.

She put her eyes at us lik' she gon' cut us down

And sayz nicely, "Well, we ain't gon' go der, is we?"

Y'all aw'ta memba wen we had'ta go and git

Dem false teefs outta de cup? I memba tellin'

One'a aw'wa Auntees, "I'll wash yo legs;

I'll rub yo feets,

But der ain't no way,

I gon' mess wit' yo teets."

Daisee be sayin', "Gurl, I nos who you talkin' 'bout.

But we ain't gon' go der, is we?"

See dis here why we come ta dis place of fam'liness.

Daisee ax, "Wen y'all gon' come back?"

Irma Jean tellz her, "You no, de same rode dat brung us here,

Is the same rode dat kin take you rat up ta aw'wa front do';

Itz de sam ' mount'a milez

E-zer way."

Sum thangs don' change cents we wuz li'l

Photograph by Ian Bernard

Lik' de way ta your city limits.

And uhm glad dat der sum thangs dat ain't.

I wuz born by de riva, in a lil' tent
Oh jest lik' de riva, I be'n runnin' ever cents,
Itz be'n'a long, a long time comin'
But I 'no a change gon' com oh yeez, it will.

growing

a time to lead and be led

Everything in me

Before you appeared, I walked as if
My feet were stuck in a muddy, flooded field;
I held my head down as if
Looking for pennies on a sidewalk;
Resigned to live without love,
Afraid to trust anyone with any of my skeletons,
My heart became homeless
Trying to live a livable life.
Then one morning,
In your rearview mirror,
You looked at me with a boyish grin.
Your face, full of so many colors
I wanted to just crawl inside
And look at the world from behind your eyes.
Your hair, streaks of lightning
Mixed with obsidian black strands
Fell down your back like corn silk.
Your eyes were bright like the beginning of a day
And everything in me, thanks you.
Something sweet about you lives
In the air I breathe and
As quietly as snow lays down,
You caress me with devoted hands
In undisturbed rhythm
That causes my emotions to
Weaken until I pass out.

Words are no longer trapped in my throat

As we weave into the stillness of evening.

You embrace me with arms

That rock me like a baby and

Your energetic smile

Puts a match to every part of me

And heats my blood.

And everything in me, thanks you.

Your voice, sweet and hard like new berries,

Makes me moan until I am soft and wet

Where you are hard and strong.

Our skins shine like taffeta and when

Joy rolls through me like waves, my mouth

Stretches open in a silent scream that

Blossoms like a flower.

Though we are no longer new to each other

Bedsprings cry like a legion of crickets.

We move slowly and

Savor the flavor of all that we are and sometimes,

Delay our summit

As if it was a cherished reward.

Your lips

Pressed against mine,

Produce electricity that

Inches up my thighs and

Makes

Laughter roar between my legs.

And when you touch me

Like a blind man reading Braille

I try to run away

From eye-rolling pleasures but

They chase me

Until I can't run any more.

And everything in me, thanks you.

Laughter

Like the sound of many rivers

Heading for the Gulf

Emerges

From deep inside

When you are near and

Whenever I feel

Your skin against mine,

My brain

Curls up

Like wilted leaves and

I stumble

Like a broken toy.

And I guess you know by now,

Everything in me

Thanks you.

Rain

The land waits for rain and
I wait for you to
Whisper my name softly; to
Wet my hair with tears
From the corner of your eye; to
Fill a naked need in mine; to
Kiss me until I
Perspire then
Quiet the river that
Rages between my hips that
Beg to let loose its moan; to
Make love
Flow through me like hot lava.
I wait for you to
Ease the throbbing of my heart
With a touch that
Opens my eyes, filters the past and
Lets in the future. A touch that
Inspires freedom to ring in my soul.
I wait for you to
Hold me with hands, big and careful
That know what they want to
Touch; help me to
Understand why the feel your skin
Makes me forget to inhale and exhale.

I wait for you to

Make melodies

Lose their temper and

Pass through me like an arrow; and when I

Emerge from a cloud of fatigue, and

Fill the air with soft grunts, I

Haul my dreams

Into the waking world and

Dance in the wind until I can

Go to a place

Where there's enough silence to

Absorb all of you.

My heart pounds

Whenever I relive how we combined

The power of my womanness with

The strength of your manness.

When I look into your eyes and feel

'The something' in my eyes

That wasn't there before,

It makes my toes

Curl and uncurl and

Curl and spread open and

When I pass out, you revive me

Again and again

As we dig into each other

Like loose earth; we

Receive and

Breathe each other the way

Gray waves roll in from the Gulf and

Take back

Fragrances we created; we

Rise and fall

In a steady rhythm the way tides

Listen and obey the moon's mood.

I wait for you to

Squeeze my eyes shut with joy; to

Plant more memories

Before these

Settle like dust on a road; and to

Free my screams and

Let them slash through years.

I wait for you

The way the land waits for rain.

lagniappe

Under the Oaks

May 1995. New Orleans. 5000 Block St. Charles Avenue. Veranda of a Victorian era library.

As typical for late spring, the afternoon air was warm, muggy and felt like another layer of skin. There was little respite from the relentless sun beneath the mammoth shadows cast by the wind-sculpted oaks in the Garden District.

Barely a breeze stirred as 'Word Warriors,' a feisty posse of poets, and Meleena, a local flutist, were summoned by muse Euterpe to perform at a library benefit.

Meleena, Amazon-like in stature, resourceful and an instigator with a lullaby soothing voice.

The Warriors. Dalencia, average height and charismatic, possessed a voice as penetrating as a riverboat whistle, was our leader and spokesperson. Julea, even-tempered, petite and soft-spoken was the embodiment of femininity. My name is Mavielle, often described as daring and always assumed to be in need of medication whenever my playfulness pushed a button.

The events of this day tested the bonds of girlfriendom and revealed some things best kept close to our own hearts.

Before any talk of a party or 'renting' a date, our energies were focused on delivering a memorable performance.

11:00. Word Warriors arrived at the library excited as first graders on a field trip. We joked and laughed as we transported our equipment like an army of ants.

"Dalencia, will you grab my backpack from the front seat of my car, please, ma'am?" I shouted from behind the stage.

"While you're at, can you bring my purse, please?" Julea added.

"Oookay," she replied, eyes squinting in the bright sun. "Mavielle, what in the world do you have in this backpack?" she asked, pretending to strain.

"A pistol, a pair of panties, a pack of condoms, and a pouch of instant grits," I joked.

"Please, not one of those days!" she huffed and puffed, rolling her eyes.

"Too late, it's already one of those days!" Julea said, staggering and groping for a chair or something to balance herself. "My sugar must be up again because my head is spinning like a top. The last time I had it checked, it registered 121."

"That is high. So, if a sour-puss was to nibble at your neck, would that bring it down? You know, the way sweet notes drown out sour ones," I offered as an elementary observation while helping her to sit down.

"I'll be all right, Mavielle. Aren't we a pair?" she said, leaning back with her eyes to the sky. "I'm high sugar. And you're low," she kidded.

"So does that make us a Hi-Lo combo?" I asked, laughing.

"Julea, if you would like, we can change the line-up so that you can read after me," Dalencia suggested.

"I just need a moment to settle down, that's all," she replied.

"Yep, it's going to be one of those days," Dalencia repeated as our pre-show playtime ended.

Ten Minutes of Fame

High noon and it's not okay at this corral. After Meleena reviewed our line-up, she discovered during sound check that one of her amps malfunctioned. She dialed two numbers and within fifteen minutes a more powerful amp was delivered. She was determined to start the program on time. And she did.

1:00. Show Time. One last tug at her tastefully form-fitted salmon-colored dress, Meleena put on a manufactured smile then sashayed like a runway model towards center stage. The vibration of her footsteps made the mic rock unsteady.

"Good afternoon. My name is Meleena," she bellowed confidently, grabbing the mic like a rock star.

"Good afternoon, Meleena," the audience responded like elementary students greeting their principal at morning assembly. Their curious eyes were fixed on her like a hungry heron on small fish.

"Welcome to the 12th Annual Tremé Book Benefit. I'm your Mistress of Ceremony. We are fortunate to have with us today, 'Word Warriors.' I've seen these ladies in action and let me tell you, they are awesome! So sit back and let them stir your creative juices and satisfy your artistic appetites and maybe fly you to the moon while they're at it. They told me to say that," she said, cocking her head and wrinkling her nose.

"Before Word Warriors come up, I would like to perform a piece I recently composed. The little things I love most about New Orleans inspired what you're about to hear."

Meleena raised her flute, closed her eyes and blew pieces of her soul into the muggy air. The first group of notes hung like echoes that waited for the others to join this particular New Orleans second-line. She bowed as the audience rewarded her with a standing ovation that made her shine like a 'beacon' to seafaring vessels in dense fog.

"Thank you very much!" she shouted as her voice was challenged by the loud hum of a crowded streetcar on its rusty tracks.

"Please give a warm welcome to Dalencia as she introduces her posse," she requested between a lull in street noise and river traffic. They passed each other slow and careful like two 18-wheelers going in opposite directions on a narrow country road.

"Thank you. Meleena you were awesome! Let's give it up again for our MC," Dalencia solicited more applause.

The audience obliged then resumed fanning their moist faces with our programs.

"My name is Dalencia and no doubt Meleena's a tough act to follow but we hope that you will enjoy *our* presentation," she said, standing stiff-legged behind the mic.

"Thank you for flying with Word Warriors. Please take a moment and direct your attention to the left side of the stage. There you will see a couple of not-so-nervous looking ladies who are ready to serve their poetic delicacies. Dinner will not be served during this short flight but please feel free to quench your thirsts as we don't want anyone to dehydrate," she said, imitating a flight attendant.

"First we have a focused Julea," Dalencia said, beckoning her to take a bow.

Julea moved forward, waved her hand like a member of the royal family, showed off her luscious red fingernails, bowed then stepped back like an obedient child.

"Don't let her petite appearance fool you. You're in for a *big* surprise," she said, rubbing her hands together in anticipation.

"And we also have Mavielle," she said, letting out a long sigh.

"Present!" I yelled like a kindergartner answering roll-call.

"You'll have to excuse Mavielle. She's the joker in our deck of poets. Sometimes she behaves like she's not all here, but she is. And hopefully, someone has had her medication and will mind herself," she teased, stretching her eyes in my direction.

"And we are 'Word Warriors.' So, sit back, relax and enjoy our presentation on love," she said, waving her hand like Queen Zulu on Mardi Gras Day.

She closed her eyes, swayed to music audible only to her then recited her poems as if the words were written inside of her lids.

"Thank you very much," she said, bowing and soaking up her ten minutes of fame. "And now for your listening pleasure, please give your attention to Julea."

Julea entered the stage and walked towards her like a graduating senior to receive her diploma.

"Thank you, Dalencia," she responded, tip-toeing to the mic. She inhaled and exhaled, closed her eyes, then released her soulful messages that seeped into the nooks and crannies of our consciences. As she exited the stage amid a thunderous applause, all eyes followed her like bouncing balls. The energy she emitted seemed to repel marauding mosquitoes in search of hot blood.

"Whoa! I said you were in for a big surprise," Dalencia said, seeking more applause. "Julea, you left so much electricity up here I may have to bottle it and take it home," she blurted, pretending to get a jolt from the mic.

"Last, but not least, is Mavielle. And as I said before, I don't know what to expect but here she is, our runaway child," she announced, extracting more laughter.

"*Runaway child, running wild*,' I better go back home, quoting a musical quote from the Temptations. I do apologize for my singing or lack of it. I reckon I'm the Mavielle that Dalencia so eloquently described. Before I begin, is it all right with you if I slipped off these high heels?"

"No," the audience responded.

"Being so short, I get kissed a lot on the forehead. And so I started wearing high heels. It's a country girl thing," I enunciated slowly in southern drawl.

"I wrote this first piece in honor of my mother who was creative, self-taught and confident," I explained. The poem drew approving nods, knowing smiles and sympathetic tears from the older women.

"Now and then, folks say to me, 'You don't sound like you're from New Orleans.' And I've been meaning to ask, 'How does someone from New Orleans sound?'" I rambled to Dalencia's displeasure as I rifled my papers for something contextually lighter.

"People from New Orleans tend to make shortcuts of words," a young woman blurted as hands around her shot into the air like missiles.

"Like 'Hayadoin' instead of, "How are you doing?" and "Hayamamadem" instead of, 'How's your mom and the rest of the family?' Ever wonder why?"

"Laziness?" the same woman replied.

"Think of it as time management. If you had one second to ask a question, which is quicker, 'hayamamadem' or 'How's your mom and the rest of the family?'"

"Are you fixin' to make groceries, Mavielle?" Dalencia heckled, looking at her watch.

"You can call me Mustang Sally if'n you want to Ms. D.," I delivered each word as slow as poured molasses on a cold morning on a stack of hot flapjacks.

Oh, no she didn't call you out! my inner voice echoed.

"You don't look like a mustang to me," Dalencia retorted.

"Just for that I'm going to explain how I got that nickname."

She stretched her eyes and pretended to choke herself.

"Would you all mind if I was to explain how I got that nickname?" I asked in southern drawl.

"No!" the audience shouted.

"Well, my daddy was the first to call me Mustang Sally 'cause I was perty quick gettin' away from *many* well-deserved whuppin's. I used to shimmy up the pine tree in our front yawd more faster than squirrels. And one of the other reasons, I got that nickname," I said, pausing, looking at an anxious Dalencia. "I reckon I best be moving along 'cause Ms. D. looking at me mighty frightful over yonder. Y'all have been great. I appreciate your indulgences," I said, exiting.

"Ah, what was the other reason?" someone from the audience shouted.

Dalencia stared at me, pressed her lips tightly together and beckoned me to exit the stage immediately. I did not respond.

"How about that Mavielle! I think she better slow that Mustang down," Dalencia said, neighing.

"On behalf of Word Warriors, 'Thank You.' We hope that you enjoyed our presentation and perhaps we'll see you at one of our future programs. And now back to our MC, hereee's Meleena," she said, handing the mic off like a baton in a relay race.

"Have you enjoyed yourselves so far?!" Meleena asked, riding the wave of enthusiasm.

"Yes!" their shouts penetrated the evergreen hedges that separated the library from the Avenue.

"Let's give it up again for 'Word Warriors!'" she hollered.

"The benefit is not over. Tonight, there'll be an auction *and* a party*. So we invite you to bring a guest, your checkbooks, your credit cards, and your cash to support a worthy cause. Thank you. You've been a great audience. See *you* tonight," Meleena announced, then left the stage.

As the audience applauded and slowly dispersed, we huddled backstage and assessed our presentation and feedback.

"Dalencia, Mavielle, you ladies rocked! You had them laughing so hard, they cried," Meleena said, joining our post-presentation meeting.

"That was strictly improv and Mavielle's lack of medication," Dalencia smirked.

"Whatever. You guys were awesome! And the audience loved you. And you, Ms. Julea!" she said, shaking her head in awe. "You dared any of us to sidestep our moral responsibility to one another. And you definitely weren't shy about bringing into the open something so many keep buried. I certainly felt empowered to face my demons and I'm positive everyone else did," Meleena complimented with an approving nod.

"Thank you. I've learned firsthand that it's harder to remain silent than to speak up," Julea replied, eyes watering.

"It takes a lot of courage to do that piece," I said, hugging.

"You were also awesome, Meleena," Dalencia mentioned.

"Yes, you were," Julea and I concurred.

"We'll have to do this again," Meleena offered.

"Same time next year?" Dalencia suggested.

"Maybe before. We still have the party tonight," she reminded.

Conflict

"So, Meleena, uh, what about this *party*?" I inquired.

"Are you coming?" she asked.

"Sure. But I don't have a date and I don't want to come stag."

"There's nothing wrong with coming stag. I do it sometimes," Dalencia interrupted, shaking her shoulders from side to side.

"You have a husband and therefore a choice about when and when not to come stag," I replied, snapping my fingers.

"It's no big deal. If it will make you comfortable, I'll even come stag. That way, you won't have to feel so *a*-lone," Dalencia enunciated, stretching her lips.

"You just confirmed what I said. Besides, it's not the same," I said, opening my palms to the sky. "So, do you have a single friend I can invite to escort me to the party tonight?"

"Mmm. No fever," she said, touching my forehead with the back of her hand. "Maybe an exotic bug bit you and the venom has finally affected your mind. Because there is no way, I'll hook you up with *any*body," she replied, bobbing her head.

"I t'awght we were *frwends,*" I said, lowering my head like a naughty child.

"We are Mavielle. But friends don't ask friends to do what you're asking."

"I didn't ask to rent one of your friends. I could look in the yellow pages for that. Anyway, if I can't ask my friends whom should I ask? A stranger?"

"If that's what you want to do then knock yourself out," she responded, shaking her head like a dashboard Hula doll.

Sensing a catfight, Meleena moved between us like a boxing referee.

"Julea, are you coming to the party?" Meleena asked.

"I don't know yet. I may have to work tonight. But I'll let you know as soon as I find out," she explained.

"Ladies. Ladies. I need to know who's coming and if you're bringing a guest. That way, I'll know how many comps to request," Meleena said, squeezing the sides of her head to release tension.

"Wow! We get comps?!" I exclaimed.

"Yep. In appreciation of your outstanding performance, the benefit committee wanted you to have them," she replied.

"Count me in, plus one," Dalencia responded, grinning.

"Count me in, plus one, too," I said confidently.

"Put me down and I'll let you know when I get home. That's the best that I can do," Julea said, hunching her shoulders.

Meleena left with the number of comps needed and returned a few minutes later grinning as if she had just eaten the best meal of her life.

"Good news! We each get two comps. One for you and one for a guest," she advised, handing out the VIP packets.

"Thank you, Ms. Meleena," we replied like bright-eyed first graders getting a tasty snack after naptime.

"Thank you, ladies," she responded then headed behind the stage to repack her gear.

Dalencia and I resumed a friendly squabble.

"Well, Mavielle, you didn't have to be soo—."

"Honest?" I replied, raising my brows.

"I was going to say unstable," she said, sticking out her tongue.

"It's okay if you don't want to hook me up with one of your friends."

"What part of 'no' don't you understand? Is it the 'n' or the 'no'?! You should be thinking about our next gig?" she said, redirecting my attention.

"Well, *my* next gig is *getting* a date for the *party* tonight."

"Mavielle, will you give it a break?!"

"How soon we forget! We have a radio interview with 'Big Jake' next week, remember?" I responded, stretching my eyes aware of her diversionary tactic.

"Are you going?"

"No. But, don't worry about me," I replied, twisting my lips.

"*Don't worry about a thing. 'Cause every little thing, gonna be all right–*" she sang, taunting and actually torturing me.

"I won't bother you about an escort if you *promise* not to sing."

"I can do that. If you can."

"So, did you tell Julea or Meleena about my proposition?"

"No, I did not tell them about your *craziness*," she growled.

"Okay. I'll ask them myself. I'm certain *one* of them *may* have a single friend they wouldn't mind my asking to the party."

"Good for them," she snarled.

"One of the benefits of coming stag, I get to dance with *whomever* and even enjoy the stares of guys with their girls *by* their sides. Of course, with a hook-up, I'll be so quiet you wouldn't know that I'm around."

"Listen, if I hooked you up with one of my friends and something went wrong, I'd feel bad," she clarified.

"That was all you had to say in the beginning. Besides, I was just kidding. I'm not that desperate to beg or rent a date."

"Well, I hope you enjoyed yourself."

"I just wanted to see how far you would go to help a friend."

"I have my limits," she replied, looking over my head.

"Yes, I see. You have your limits. I should have also. Do you remember when you wanted to get your dance on?"

"What about it?" she inquired all cocky.

"I wasn't in the mood to go out that night and probably should not have, but *you* felt like dancing. And because I consider us to be friends, I didn't limit myself in that regard."

"And your point is?"

"My point is. I got dressed. Left the cozy comfort of *my* home. Went to a club. *Inhaled* second-hand smoke so *you* could get your dance on!"

"And I said, 'Thank you.' Didn't I?!" she snarled.

"Yes, you did, but—"

"But what? What you're asking me is more extreme than going dancing."

"More extreme? What could be more *extreme* than going to a club where *two* people were *shot*? Or having someone follow you! You don't think that's extreme?"

"You told me that you managed to lose the guy."

"But what if I hadn't?" I said, shaking my head in disbelief. "I didn't know him or even approach him. But if you've never been stalked," I said, eyes welling up, "I can't make you understand what that feels like."

"All right, Mavielle. You've made your point"

Plan B

The intrigue of an escort, paid or unpaid, was a fleeting thought that grabbed me the way chewed gum on a hot sidewalk stuck to shoes.

I took matters into my own hands.

"Dalencia, I have a date for the party tonight. So let's not allow this thing to cause a rift between us, okay?"

"Okay. So who's your date?"

"Do you see that guy over there in the yellow tee-shirt with the Tasmanian Devil on the front?" I mouthed through clenched teeth.

"I don't see anybody. Have you been in the sun too long?"

"The one with the wrinkled khaki shorts, black ribbed socks, brown shoes with black shoelaces, green-rimmed glasses, standing over there near the side gate," I said, mimicking a ventriloquist.

"I still don't see who you're talking about," she stretched her neck looking over my head.

"Here, take this program and pretend we're in a deep discussion. You look at my paper and I'll look at yours then I'll get a good idea where the guy is and let you know."

Our heads bobbed like floaters in the water attached to a fishing pole going from paper to the vicinity of the stranger.

"The guy standing near the chair where the blue backpack is. Now do you see him?" I whispered.

In an awkward moment, my eyes met the stranger's looking at me trying not to look at him. I watched as Dalencia's eyes moved from the backpack up towards the stranger's face.

"Are you serious?! He's—he's," she said, snapping her fingers as if to break an imaginary spell.

"He's what?" I asked, dropping my head like it was heavy, daring her to beat down my enthusiasm.

"He's—," she stuttered, blinking as if a loose hair had gotten stuck in the corner of her eye.

"He will be my date tonight!"

"Mavielle, I'm more certain now than ever that you forgot to take your medicine," she insinuated, her eyes flaring like red jewels.

"What's with this medication thing? I'm not into drugs. I don't need to swallow any pills *or* inhale any smoke *or* sniff any powder *or* drink any spirits. I am alert and oriented."

"Oh, no! Now the girl thinks she's Oriental," she kidded, touching her forehead, faking a fainting spell.

"Drama, drama."

Okay, you wrote a check. Now you have to cash it. What are you going to say to the stranger? Don't you feel a little awkward? Why don't you just smile and keep going right pass him! Uh, oh. Now what are you going to do? It's too late! He's seen you. Time to put up or shut up! my inner voice interrogated as I casually strolled towards the colorfully-dressed stranger.

"Hi. I hope you enjoyed the program," I said, using our presentation as an ice breaker.

"It was ve-ry nice. Yes, I enjoy you poetries ve-ry much," he whispered, shaking my hand as if it was light as brushed cotton.

His smile stretched across his face the way the GNO spanned the Mississippi River to connect the Eastbank to the Westbank. And the way he looked at me made my insides swirl like a feather dancing in a whirlpool.

Don't just stand there and rock the boat. Rob this cradle, girl! these words of encouragement from my inner voice plowed my night with hope.

I detected an accent that made me *ooo la-la* slowly melt inside like expensive dark chocolate.

Lagniappe! Aren't you glad you paid attention to Ms. Goudeau au lycée? He's cute. This might work, my inner counselor inquired.

"So you really enjoyed the program?" I repeated.

Okay my conscious counterpart, you wrote a poem that drew tears out of hiding but you can't come up with something more original than 'I hope you enjoyed the program?' Breathe and get creative.

"Yes," he chirped, smiling from deep down where it counted.

Our eyes were fixed on each other like those of a 4 year old on the countertop where nickel candy and penny bubble gum were in sight but out of reach.

Go girl! You got a bite! Not too much pressure. Give him some slack! Now reel him in! You fished for a date with your friend but she refused to help. What could you lose by asking this stranger? You may not have an

*appetite for the socially unpopular older woman-younger man phenomenon.
Don't let that stop you. How many times have you seen Dracula bite older
women? All right then. Get a move on.*

"You want to come to a party with me tonight?" I asked,
imitating Arnold of *Diff'rent Strokes*.

"Yes," he whispered as if a secret was caught in his throat.

His eyes sparkled like the *good stuff* brought out on special
occasions. He neutralized my rough tone with a smile that moved
across his face the way the sun splashed into a gray morning sky.

Trees, on opposite sides of the Avenue with their protruding
branches, touched each other like "London Bridge is all built up."
Under the shadow of these monstrous oaks, we sat facing each other
as our chairs sunk deeper into the thick St. Augustine lawn. In our
little world, the way life commanded dreams on snowy nights; we
worked out the details of our rendezvous.

Dalencia and the others gawked at us with sharp eyes and
perky ears. They were close enough to see our faces but far enough
not to hear our conversation. If they were flies on a wall or ants in the
lawn, they could have buzzed around our heads or crawled up our
legs to hear our plans.

"The tickets are $25. Be at the front gate at 7:30," I explained,
shaking my finger at him like a scolding mother.

"Yes," he whispered as if confronted by a playground tyrant.

I could have repeated the same instructions ten times and it
would not have mattered. I didn't know what else to say so I
reviewed our arrangements. He smiled like a child with a new toy as
we stood and went our separate ways.

*This must be one of those instances where a man's touch can make
you forget to breathe,* my inner voice observed. *Your brain stalled and
apparently slipped gears because you didn't ask his name. Now, you don't
know where he lives. You have no way of calling him or tracking him down.*

In less time that it took to write a check or clip coupons from
Sunday's paper, Dalencia pounced to extract information about the
stranger. The others were on her heels, staring at me like fresh road-
kill.

"Mavielle's got a boyfriend," they taunted.

*Smile girl, they'll think you're up to something. That would be
Nana's advice to you, right?* my inner voice interjected. I smiled though
on the inside, I shivered like leaf in a brisk November wind.

"Dalencia, I took your hint and invited a stranger," I said, rearing back on my heels.

"That was your doing, Mavielle. I didn't give you any hint."

"Would you like an instant replay of that conversation?"

"No need. I know what I said. So what were you and that guy talking about?"

"Do you remember a little bird saying something like, 'When I find a date, you're going to want to know all about it?"

"You don't have to be like that," she sighed.

"Well, Mavielle, you've outdone yourself this time. It's too late. The man is gone!" Julea taunted, having fully recovered from an earlier spike in blood sugar.

"I guess you have a date, huh?!" Dalencia instigated.

I ignored them as my inner voice deduced. *Meleena has a date. Dalencia has a date. Julea could have a date, if she wanted. And you approached your friends to hook you up. And they wouldn't help, so you helped yourself. But a stranger?*

The voice pounced harder. *Remember your senior prom? When you couldn't get a date and the one guy you did ask said the only way he'd go with you would be if he could do whatever he wanted to you? Remember when you threatened to break his arms and relocate his kneecap?*

The voice echoed louder. *You remember when you made your début? Who escorted you to the cotillion? That's right, your baby brother! And then he didn't want to do that stupid waltz with you and left you standing in the middle of the dance floor.*

The voice explored further. *And remember Albert? That guy who played football with you and your brothers? The one who admitted to squeezing your breast on the pretense of tackling you to keep you from scoring a touchdown? And what did you, our little Wonder Woman, do? You hauled off and slapped him so hard, he grinned for two months. The guy had nerves of steel to get up afterwards. And you remember what he told you years later? "It was worth it." You were pretty rough then and that same mentality followed you straight into womanhood.*

"Don't you have a date with that guy?" Meleena asked, propping her hands on her hips like a mother about to give an embarrassing lecture.

"I don't know what you're talking about."

"Are you looking for backup?" she inquired.

"No. But I was hoping to get an extra ticket for my girlfriend, Nana and her friend."

"Yeah, right. You should go home right now and take your meds," she suggested.

"Gotta give it to you, Mavielle. You are daring, but this is *waay* over the top for you. And we'll be right here, front and center, when it's *show time*. We hope that you're going to be ready, because we are!" Dalencia teased.

"Well, in that case, I may not come!" I said, challenging their curiosities.

"You'd better show up!" Meleena threatened, wrinkling her forehead like an accordion.

"And if you don't, I'll beat down your front door and drag your sorry butt over here," Dalencia said, all cocky.

"One thing about being single and going stag, I avoid the emotional and social embarrassment of being put down by a husband or a boyfriend. I also avoid controlling and threatening stares," I said aware of their marital status.

It became so quiet, I could hear their heartbeats.

"Another thing about stag, there's no one to amend my personal constitution. Stag or *a*-lone on this past New Year's Eve, I put on my flannel PJs, lit a scented candle, added a log to the fire, sat and sipped 7-Up from a wine glass and enjoyed Sam Cooke and Jerry Butler. At the stroke of midnight, I sang *Auld Lang Syne* as fireworks and gunshot broke night's quiet and announced the beginning of the next 365-day cycle. And the topper, I didn't have to deal with a complaining husband or boyfriend."

"Aw shucks, Mavielle's in one of those non-stop 'get it off my chest' flights," Dalencia remarked.

"And one more thing, ever notice that one last leaf on a tree to fall as autumn transitions to winter?"

"How lonely?" Dalencia responded.

"It's like that half-empty/half-full scenario. Just, that last leaf, it outlived the others. It's all in how you look at a thing," I responded, smiling. "And that's all I have to say on the matter."

You sure talk to yourself a lot, don't you? my inner voice posed.

The Stranger

The anticipation of my date with the stranger raced through me like a loose javelin.

To avoid drama-rama, I reviewed the *'is there a girlfriend or wife'* checklist with input from my inner voice.

Did you notice whether anyone sat next to him? No. He could be single. Or his girlfriend could be at home. Impale that thought. Did you see a ring or a ring shadow on his third finger, left hand? No. So he could be single. Embrace that possibility! Here's opportunity.

"Mavielle, that guy you were talking to, he's a little on the *thin* side, don't you think?" Dalencia instigated.

"I likes my man like I likes my bread. *Thin*-sliced," I replied confidently punctuating my preference.

"Well, you should *loove* him. So what's his name?"

"I don't remember," I said, exercising selective amnesia.

"So what does he do? Is he married? Does he have a girlfriend? Is he gay?"

"Let's see. Don't ask. Won't tell."

"I don't know if you've noticed or not but he's *white.*"

"Is that what this is all about that he's white? It's not that he's *thin* but that he's *white*? Is this a problem." I responded, not hiding my salty disposition. For the first time, I felt alienated from my creative cohort as if I had been evicted from our culture.

"It's not a problem for me. It could be one for you. So what does he do? Is he married? Does he have a girlfriend?" she asked, avoiding my eyes, focusing on her fishing expedition.

"He's not interviewing for a job."

"For all that you know he could be a bank robber."

"Well, if he's a bank robber, at least he'll have money and I won't have to pay for the date, will I?"

"Then I'll visit you at Central Lockup when you get picked up with him because somebody recognized his post office glamour shot from the 'Most Wanted' magazine!"

"So what about *your* single friends, are any of *them* bank robbers?"

"We're not talking about my friends. We're talking about this stranger."

"As far as this stranger, it's not the color of the skin that makes a person who he or she is. It's the color of the heart. Besides, I'm not closed-minded or emotionally limited in embracing another culture," I stated my position, squinting as if blinded by the sun instead of anger.

"That's not what I meant. What I wanted to say was *remember* where you are and who you are."

"I know who I am. I know where I am. I also know that it's a sad commentary on humanity when the outside of a person matters more than the inside. I know who I am and get reminded every time I walk down a street *or* get onto an elevator *or* leisurely browse in a store *or* step outside of my door. And there are people who make sure that I don't forget. But I didn't expect you to be one of them. You've been like a sister to me but right now, I feel let down. But I'll get over it," I said, disappointed.

"Mavielle, I'm sorry. I don't want my friend, who's like a sister," she said rubbing her heart, "to get hurt. That's all."

"Just like one of your friends could have hurt me, right?"

"I don't think they would have."

"But what's different in this case? It's okay for us to embrace diversity *on* stage not *off*? And if that's not the case, convince me."

"I don't think you'll listen, if I did."

A black woman and a white man together was frowned upon in New Orleans, most southern cities and, apparently, in our little creative circle.

Regardless, I had a date that I intended to keep it.

Deva's Den

Her name's Debra but affectionately known as 'Nana' by those in her inner-inner circle. Friends for over eighteen years, our relationship evolved as true sisters. She rose early most Saturdays, ran errands for the elderly, helped single moms with their babies, and delivered food to the shut-ins. She's also renowned for her bare-faced bluntness and colorful vocabulary which has been temporarily disconnected.

"Hi, Nana. It's Mavielle!" I said in a breaking news voice.

"I do have caller ID and know who you are. *Unless you* don't know what number *you* dialed. Hey girl, what's up?"

"Can't put anything over on you, huh, Ms. CIA or Ms. FBI?"

"Either one, I can track you down better than a bugging device in your brain, tell you where you've been, how long you were there and who you talked to. So, what have you done now?"

"You're Ms. CIA, you tell me. And I *know* you're not implying that I only call when I want something."

"No, I *didn't* imply anything. I just came out and *said* what I had to say. Anyway, I hear something naughty in your voice and you *knows* how much I *likes* juicy gossip," she said, laughing.

"Nothing naughty here."

"How long have I known you?" she asked, testing my knowledge.

"How long do you think?"

"Somebody itching for a slapping ta-day!" she exclaimed.

"Okay, I'll play along. We've known each other some umpteen years and counting."

"And if you want to keep counting, I suggest you tell me what's up."

"Yes, Nana dearest."

"How many times have I told you to stop calling me that? It's Deva. D-e-v-a. De-va, with a capital 'D' as in 'Don't mess with me.'"

"Okay, Ms. 'Don't mess with me' De-va. I have a little dilemma."

"I updated my resumé last week and I don't think I put mind-reader on it. So are you going to tell me or what?"

"I need some moral support. Is it okay for me to come over?"

"Are you coming today or next year?"

"I'll be over before you're done boiling eggs for potato salad."

I arrived at Deva's house, a modest shotgun, mid-way Lapeyrouse Street and a few blocks from the Circle Food Store at St. Bernard and N. Claiborne Avenues. The chain-link fence that surrounded her house stood taller than the shortest NBA player.

"Guess what I did today?" I asked, smiling as I walked up the steps towards her.

"You farted and came over to tell me how good it felt?"

"How did you guess?"

"Look girl, my head is still spinning like a merry-go-round on speed. I'm in no mood for any craziness today." Through hung-over eyes, she warned, "You best be getting to the point 'cause I'm operating on a short fuse. I could tell by your voice that you did something that's beyond your usual."

"You make it sound like I robbed a bank or something."

"Ba-bay, if you robbed a bank, I know you better throw some of those *Forgive my French* dollars my way considering all we've been through. And don't *haave* me come and hunt you down like a cockroach on vacation," she said, snapping her fingers.

"Where do cockroaches go on vacation?"

"Hold on, *lemme* close my door and sit down," she said, laughing with anticipation. "Okay, now I'm ready. Lemme hear what brought you to Dr. Deva's," she muttered, plopping down on her sofa, pretending to take notes.

"Wait. Wait. Lemme go to the bathroom so I don't pee on myself. This sounds like it's gonna be more juicy than a Popsicle in the microwave!" she exclaimed, jumping up like a scared rabbit in hunting season. She made tracks down her long, narrow hallway, slippers slapping at the bottoms of feet.

"What I have to say is not even hotter than a six-shooter. Well, anyway. Today at the library," I said, clearing my throat.

"I'll be right there! Don't get started without me! I want to hear e-ve-ry-thang!"

"I sure hope you're not going to be in there *too* long. You know how short my attention span is since that concussion."

"Girl, this medicine I'm on got me peeing like a faucet," she said, returning to the living room out of breath.

"As I was saying before *your* bladder interrupted."

"I could have peed on your shoes. But I don't think you wanted that."

"Let's not get into medicinal side effects or bodily functions. As I was saying, I got an invitation to a party tonight."

"So what's the problem?"

"It's not a problem. It's a situation."

"Oh, Lord, I don't know if I'm ready for this, but I'll ask anyway, 'What's the situation?'"

"I approached Dalencia about hooking me up with one of her single friends for the party tonight."

"Oh, no, you didn't! Weren't you paying attention to Deva 101: *We Get Asked. We Don't Ask*? Why would you do something like that?" she said, waving her hand like a magic wand as if to undo what I did.

"I was kidding at first. Regardless, she said she wouldn't because she didn't want to feel responsible if something happened."

"I go along with that," she said, taking sides.

"So, I approached a stranger in the audience and invited him to be my date."

"You did what! Don't *haave* me get a dart gun and shoot your butt then Fed-Ex your behind to the moon," she threatened.

There was a moment of silence before we laughed.

"I invited a guy from the audience to be my date tonight," I repeated confidently.

"I heard you the first time! What drugs were you on? Better yet, did you take your *don't do stupid things* pill today? If you haven't, I have a couple here just in case somebody, a little short in the Brain Department, stopped by," she kidded.

"What's the harm? It's not like I'm going to run off and elope with this guy. We're just going to hang out *at* the party *at* the library, that's all."

"Oh, Lord, my friend done lost her mind!"

"P-lease."

"What po-zessed you to do something like that? And without me!"

"What?!" I said, but not really surprised.

"Girl, you know Deva likes to do different *thaangs*."

"To answer your question, I asked the guy in the audience because I didn't want to go *this* party stag."

"You could've invited me. Free food! How many times have I told you to call me so we can get our eat-on?"

"Two?"

"If you would have called me, I would have run by the thrift store, picked up something nice, and took my Tina Turner wig to this party! What kind of music they having at this party anyway?" she rambled like someone hit the fast-forward button.

"I believe, classical."

"Classy?"

"Three words, clas-si-cal!"

"Who's playing?"

"A pianist and a cellist."

"Did you say a p****?"

"Get your mind out of the gutter. I said a pianist."

"Well, that party sounds too boring for me to paint my toenails."

"My concern is not with who's playing at this party, it's about bringing a better impression than the one I left behind. And it involves a man."

"Don't it always? Sometimes it's better to go places alone. Just think of all of the new people you get to meet. Think of all the trouble you can stir up. Think of all the fun you can have without being on somebody's leash. But if you go with somebody, you'd have to stay closer to him than his own shadow. Last time I looked in the mirror, I had only two legs, I don't bark but I'll bite the fool out of somebody if they try to put some leash on me."

"I wanted a date. What's so wrong with that?"

"I feel'ya. You remember that 71 year old DJ who tried to pick us up?" she said, changing the subject.

"I thought he was just showing four women that he could handle them on the dance floor one-by-one or by twos."

"And he did. And he loved every minute of it! Thinking he was getting his toast buttered on two sides by four women!"

"Do you remember that spunky 86 year old king of the Illinois coronation?"

"Do I ever! That old ta-ta nearly died when he had you on one side and me on the other like he was crunchy peanut butter between two slices of honey wheat bread."

"Now, Deva, whenever you tell that story, make sure to mention that we were on stage, dressed in evening gowns waiting to take pictures with the king."

"Sometimes it's good to leave out *certain* details. That's how you peak interest and start rumors," she said, blowing at her forefinger like it was a pistol she had just fired. "Deva 101: Creative Lies," she mentioned, snapping her fingers. "Pay close attention next time."

"Deva, you are *soo* bad."

"I don't thing so. You're the one who asked a stranger out. How bad is that?"

"All the way to the bone?"

"There are so many 'heffas' out there who don't know jack about how to have a clean, good time. I ain't talking about opening your legs and letting Tom, Dick, Harry and their resurrected grandpas run through you like they was ordering fries at the drive thru. I'd have to tell them, 'You got me mixed up with somebody who cared,'" she explained, upset at the plight of how men and women treat each other.

"I know just what you're talking about because the first and middle names on my birth certificate do not read 'Fast Food.'"

"Miss *Thang*, I hope that you notice that I've been trying to keep my *colorful* words out of our conversation. But sometimes, I gotta get down and dirty so folks know I mean *bid-ness*."

"I used to cringe at those colorful words but now, I move over them and concentrate on what you were trying to say. But thanks for keeping it clean today. Anyway, I'm here to get a few make-up tips."

She laughed so hard she fell off the sofa.

"Did I say something to amuse you or are you exercising or maybe checking for dust bunnies under your sofa?"

"You and make-up! Ha! And how long do I have to hang on before you give me the low down on why you want make-up? Or should I give you a laxative and wait for you to get diarrhea of the mouth?"

"As I started to say," I paused, stretching my eyes at her. "Today, at the library —"

"Mavielle, tell me something other than being at some library or folks are going to read about a crazy poet who got strangled by her best friend. And if they ask me why I did it, 'I'd ask them, 'Have you ever heard Mavielle tell a story?' And, they'd say, "No." Then I'd tell them "shut up" 'cause you ain't got the brains to understand where I'm coming from. Now, are you going to tell me or do I have to get my plunger and work it out of you?"

"Okay, okay. Today at the library."

"Oh girl, don't *haave* me slap you and make you put on a straight jacket, lace it up yourself then find your way out."

"Every time you interrupt, I keep forgetting where I am!" I teased.

"Too much traffic in your head? You might need a signal light in there to control the flow. Lemme get a glass of wine! Better yet, I need the whole bottle or else I'll have to wrang your lil' skinny neck."

"While you get your wine, I'll tell you about the guy I *kind of* met," I said, aware that she would have the last word.

"How in heck can you *kind of* meet somebody? That's like saying 'oops, I kinda robbed the bank,'" she said, laughing, folding her arms. "So what's this guy's name? I might know him."

"I don't think you know him. As a matter of fact, I *know* you don't know him!"

"I know a lot of people. And *if* I *don't* know him, I'll find out everything about him *including* the color of the underwear he wore *two* years ago on Labor Day, the time of his birth and how long his mama was in labor with him! So what's his name?"

"I don't know," I said, squirming.

"Then I guess it's useless to ask if he's married, huh?"

"I guess so."

"Girl, you should take *two smart pills* before you go *anywhere* even if it's to take out the trash or press your garage door opener."

"You're a real comedian today, huh?"

"No. You're the comedian. So where are you going with this 'I don't know his name' stranger?"

"We are going to a party *at* the library *at* the library!"

"So tell me, Mavielle, is he ugly or drop-dead gorgeous?

Make Me Over?

Nana's, I mean, Deva's living room.

"What do you know about this guy?" Nana posed a legitimate question.

"Well, he's your height. Slim. Hazel eyes."

"Girl, I can get more information about 3-day old donuts than you did about some guy you're going out with."

"It'll be all right. I'm here mostly for your company. Well, almost."

"Now we're getting somewhere. My friend wants me to Devatize her, huh?"

"Aren't you the fashion police?"

"Correction. I'm the Superintendent of *All Eyes on Me!*" she said, touching her hip with one finger then making a sizzling sound. "Looking at you, I'm no miracle worker. Well, we're going to fix you up and when Deva gets done, look out all you wannabes with your highlights and inflated boobs 'cause here comes Ms. Delicious!"

"Me. Delicious?"

"Don't let that go to your head." she warned, laughing.

"I would like to look as natural as possible, nothing extreme, okay?"

"And why would you even want to?"

"What's wrong with the way I look?"

"What's wrong? What's right?"

"Here's a news flash, De-va. I got a date and wasn't wearing any make-up," I said, nodding. "Something must have appealed to him. I'm just here for a little help, not a complete make me over. Just a little advice, that's all."

"And, wwwhat time is this party?"

"7:30."

"And wwwhat time is it now?"

"4:30."

"That's not even enough time to apply foundation! Here's a little advice," she said, leaning in. "If I was the official fashion chief of police, you'd have more tickets than a meter maid. And then you'd be on house arrest until you *learned* how to coordinate a wardrobe!"

She led me to a spare bedroom that was transformed into a closet. She pulled out a key lime colored outfit and a pair of matching shoes that nearly blinded me. She opened her jewelry box and selected accessories that were not key lime but jawbreaker yellow.

"Ooo, Deva, those colors are brighter than the July sun. If I wore something like that to bed, I'd keep myself awake."

"It's all about standing out and making a statement."

"Making a statement like, 'Here I am!' Because if I wore something like that, a hit man couldn't miss me."

"Stop clowning. Now, back to the guy you kind of met. What if this guy is a bank robber?"

"He's not a bank robber!" I said confidently.

"You don't even know his name. How do you know he's not some bank robber? Doggone, I gotta pee again. See what you did?"

"You should re-train your bladder."

"Girl, I'm just playing with you. Do you remember when we walked into that Zulu party two years ago? Our hips moving before we hit the dance floor and all eyes were on us?"

"And you remember the request we got to 'turn out' a party the next night?"

"Yes, sir, buddy. They still talks about us. One guy called us the Terrible Two's. Well, anyway, I brought that up to say, 'when I get done, all eyes gone be on *you!*"

"I'm interested in two pairs of eyes, his and mine. I tend to be a little shy, you now," I said, shielding my face from her earthquake of a reaction.

"You! Shy?! P-leez."

"Well, just a little."

"If you're shy, then I'm a call girl in the castle. You shy! You asked a stranger to go out with you and you don't even know his name and now you're telling me that you're shy?!"

"Maybe, not too shy. So can you do your Deva thing? But not too much, okay?"

"Do you tell the Greyhound bus driver how to drive?" she said, dropping her make-up kit on the table.

"If I'm sitting in the front, I may."

"Just leave the driving to me."

"I don't want to look over made-up like some dead person."

"Let me tell you that 80 year old Detriot mortician can work a miracle on the dead. And I can do my thing on the living," she said laughing. "Now, would you like some Hypnotique while I work on you?"

"You mean instead of formaldehyde?"

"If you don't dilute it just right, it can put you in a trickbag."

"I pass. You know I can't drink and talk at the same time."

"Yes, I do. And I've seen up close and personal what 7-Up and the night air do to you. You are one cheap date," she said, giggling.

"How many times have I told you about my low tolerance for alcohol?"

"You seem to have a low on common sense, too but I won't go there. You and your drama."

"Just do the best you can, please ma'am. I mean, Superintendent."

"Okay, let's start with a little eye shadow."

"No. It gets into my eyes and I have trouble seeing. And I can't afford to have blurred vision tonight," I said, looking into her hand-held mirror.

"Okay, we can skip that. How about a little rouge to liven up your cheeks?" she asked, twirling the blush applicator like drumstick.

"No. It breaks me out."

"Okay, we can skip that, too. What about lipstick? Do you have a problem with it?"

"Fever blisters."

"If you can't wear eye shadow, rouge or lipstick, then I can't help you, not even a little," she said, conceding defeat.

"Never mind, just give me the works. I'll deal with the side effects later."

"Deva will have you looking so finger lickin' good the stranger will be on you like a bump on a log. I just wish I could be a fly on the wall to see his face," she interjected with newfound energy and continued to stamp me with her "Deva was here" signature. "When I get through with you, you won't recognize yourself."

"Will the stranger be able to?"

"You know what I mean."

"Yeah, I know. I'm having second thoughts about this date."

"If you don't think you're going to that boring party, then don't *haave* me waste my time trying to transform the bride of Frankenstein into a Cinderella," she said, her hands on her hips.

"It's just a matter of a little cold feet."

"You should've gotten cold feet before you invited a stranger on a date. Anyway, we're going to have all eyes on you. And what you do about them is your *bid-ness*. 'Cause I got two words about how those women are going to feel when they see you. Jeal Ous," she said, waving her hand. "I still wish I could be a fly on the wall."

"If you were a fly on the wall, somebody might have to resuscitate you," I warned.

"Seriously, Mavielle. You deserve a good time. You've taken care of a lot of people and have had to deal with a few knuckleheads. If going to this party with a stranger will make you forget what you have to deal with, then I'm happy for you."

"So now that we have this make-up business under control, what should I wear?"

"Well, something sweet and simple that won't put all of your *bid-ness* out there and at the same time, tease his imagination."

"I have a cream-colored floral wrap dress. It's soft to the touch. Sweet. Covers *all* of my assets and *it's* kind of sexy."

"Okay, and I think your hair will look nice in a French twist."

"Interesting that you said *French* twist. I believe the stranger is from France."

"Oh, you didn't tell me that! Ooo, laissez bontemps *roulez*! Well, you go girl. I'm definitely scared of you!"

"Très bien!"

"I sure hope you're not *French* cussing me."

"I have a problem hearing cuss, I mean, colorful words in English!"

"Because I'd have to check you."

"So what shoes should I wear? Sexy calf-stretching, neck-breaking high heels or something I can *run* in?"

"That depends."

"On?"

"On what he looks like and whether you want to run *from* or run *to* this stranger."

"Well, he looks a lot like MacGyver and *definitely* easy on the eyes."

"Who in the heck is MacGyver?"

"He's that guy on TV who uses whatever's available to get out of tight spots. I believe his name is Richard Dean something."

"Oh, yeah, I remember him. Girrl, he's cute! Well, in that case, if you don't think the stranger is jerk, then go for broke, wear stilettos! It wouldn't hurt to stuff your bra or get a push-up bra to enhance your upper body asset either!"

"I'm not wearing or putting any more in there than what I walked into your door with. I'm letting interest accrue naturally," I asserted, raising my brows.

"And how long have you been letting interest accrue? Because it appears that you haven't gotten much return on your investment."

"It doesn't matter. What's there is all mine."

"'Too much for one. Not enough for two.' I know you heard that before. Well, you ain't got enough for yourself."

"And your upper body assets are how much bigger than mine?" I shot back, looking under-eyed.

"I'm trying to fix you up with that 'Uh-huh, I remember you' look!"

"Why?"

"You gots to represent no matter where Mr. 'I don't know his name' Stranger is from!"

"It's just a date. We're not going any further than the party."

"That's what they all say. But you might, if you play it right. All I know is when I get through with you —"

"Yeah, I know, all eyes gone be on me. And if that's the case, I'd better work on my walk."

"Are you auditioning for the call girl club?"

"No, I'm not."

"Don't worry about it. Do like I do. I walk like I'm all that then work that hip motion and get roving eyes to go where *I* want them to go."

"I don't know about that. This is just a simple date at the library and I don't intend to go far with him."

"It's your *bid-ness* how *far* he gets and how *far* you want him to go. Who knows, you might even end up in France. Oui, Oui. Filé gumbo and Parlez-vous that!" she exclaimed, admiring her handiwork.

"Now go home and chill. And remember, if he tries anything, *call me*! I'll round up our butt-kicking posse and be there in no time."

"I got it covered baby girl. I got it covered," I said, smiling.

"Just watch he don't cover you," she cautioned.

The Party

6:00. The sun began its descent over East New Orleans. I enjoyed a relaxing bubble bath then rubbed the pear-scented lotion that Nana sneaked into a *get a man* goody bag. I slipped into my dress, eased into a pair of *get up outta here* heels and did not enhance my upper asset.

I looked into the mirror and didn't recognize myself just as Deva said. I brushed my hair until it fell behind my shoulders. *Beauty's Only Skin Deep* by the Temptations played on the radio, my inner voice advised, *Just be yourself.* In response, I toned down Deva's Make-over 101.

This was not an evening for hooker heels or to be made up beyond recognition. This was an evening of being comfortable in my own skin.

6:50. As *Cruisin'* by Smoky Robinson played, I mellowed out and merged onto I-10 and headed west towards adventure.

7:15. I arrived at the library and gave one ticket to the volunteer then walked towards the main entrance. Dalencia and Meleena stood in the food line and motioned for me to join them.

"So where's Julea?" I asked, looking around.

"She had to work," Dalencia answered through a pasted smile.

7:25. "Is that guy coming?" Meleena asked. Her question floated unanswered.

The minutes ticked away. I was pricked by a nagging inner voice, *Stood up, again!* I closed my eyes like Dorothy in Oz, discreetly clicked my heels and chanted silently, *I hope he comes. I hope he comes. I hope he comes.*

"So Mavielle, uh, where's your date?" Dalencia asked, leaning back on her heels with a condescending look.

I smiled, pretending it didn't matter. But it did.

7:30. "Oh my goodness!" Meleena said, enunciating one word at a time as if she was learning to read.

"Mavielle! Look who's at the front gate," she mumbled. Shocked, her mouth opened so wide, it could comfortably accommodate my fist.

Turning slowly toward the gate, I took a quick hit from an excited inner voice, *This is what you wanted, right? Here's opportunity. You're an older woman who knocked on a door and a younger man opened. He didn't have to come. But he's here. Go and claim your prize!*

I took one deep breath, squared my shoulders then strutted across the lawn like a proud peacock, feathers prominently displayed. I arrived at the gate in one piece, relieved that my legs didn't betray me or give out then looked at him all *ga-ga* and jelly-brained.

He stood on the outside of the gate with a smile that made me want to crawl inside, get comfortable and look at the world from behind *his* eyes. When he looked back at me, I felt my face flush with a power that flowed from the old earth. And when he touched my hand, it made my heart beat with the pulse of dancing drums.

See, you're not too old! It feels good, huh? Remember, be yourself, the sweet self, that inner voice applauded and encouraged.

"Hi. You made it," I said, smiling like a love-struck teenager.

"I give my word that I would come," the stranger replied.

Okay, girl. Breathe slowly. Don't blow any gaskets! my inner voice coached.

"My name is Mavielle."

"Ah, that is a nice name. Ma-vi-elle," he enunciated. "Yes, that is a nice name."

When he said your name, it felt like warm honey on your skin, didn't it? Look who's blushing, my inner voice teased.

"What is your name?" I asked, drooling.

"Didier," he answered as fireworks exploded in his eyes in my direction and mine in his.

"You have a nice name also. How do you say it again?"

"Di-di-er," he repeated not seem at all annoyed at my auditory challenges or short attention span.

"I have $25. Who I give the money to?"

"Keep your money. The ticket is a comp."

This could have been an easy $25 if you were that type of woman, but you weren't brought up like that. Good girl. Your home training shows. Your parents would be proud and Nana would be surprised, my inner voice affirmed.

"Pardon. Comp? What do you mean comp?"

"Comp means that the 'ticket' is free. Just about everything here tonight is free except for the wine and the auction items. Come in. Feel free to mingle and browse," I said, implying that we were not Siamese twins.

"You look ve-ry nice this e-ve-ning. Why would I browse? I am here to be with you," he clarified.

Good answer! You can replay that comment later, the inner voice and I agreed.

When he walked into that gate, we entered a world new to us and soon discovered we were as similar as we were different.

As the moon moved across the sky in a slow rhythm, we strolled by disapproving looks and ignored all of the socially unfriendly comments. Tonight, we were all that mattered and made it clear to all onlookers, 'Yes, we're together!'

"Mavielle, would you like some ve-ge-table?" he offered.

Not only did he arrange the food on a plate for us, he finger-fed me as we stood in the middle of a crowded room under a hand-painted ceiling. A few steps away, the Mayor of the city posed for pictures as his two meaty and muscular bodyguards stood around him like armed fleshy walls.

We meandered through the library as if we were the only two souls and swapped information more relevant to us than all of the books on the shelves.

"Didier," I stumbled over his name a couple of times. "I apologize for being so rough today. I've never approached anyone as I approached you."

"Ah, Mavielle. It is no problem. I do not think you were, how you, say 'rough'," he whispered, punctuating his statement with a smile.

We enjoyed a champagne high on 7-Up bubbles.

Streetcar Downtown

10:00. There were no clouds to hide the moon. The air, still thick and humid, stuck to our skins like damp silk. The streets were alive and filled with nighttime revelry.

Didier and I sat on the white wicker loveseat on the veranda and talked about our dreams and families. Inside, the auction was going well.

Look who's having a good time. So far so good, but don't bite off more than you can chew, my inner voice cautioned.

"Didier, would you like to take a streetcar ride?"

Didn't you tell Nana that you weren't going to leave the library? The little self-defense you know may be useless if he whispers something sweet in your ear, my inner voice hammered.

"Oh, that would be so ve-ry nice," he said, eyes twinkling.

We avoided Meleena and Dalencia but knew sooner or later we were destined to cross paths. Sooner or later became sooner when Dalencia went out of her way to make eye contact with me and motioned for us to come over.

"Didier. I would like you to meet two of the ladies who were also on the stage this morning."

In the shadow of the veranda, Meleena and Dalencia stood, arms folded across their chests. They resembled two "I Dream of Jeannie's" out of their bottles, ready to blink.

Despite the taunts *I was having the time of my life!* And as we got closer, Dalencia's face opened with a smile so full of essence, it seemed to alter her personality. She was bent on extracting information about the guy whom she described earlier as "thin" and "white."

"Meleena. Dalencia. This is Didier."

"Nice to meet you," Dalencia said, extending her hand to shake his. She didn't bother to say his name, but glanced at me with eyes demanding a play-by-play briefing of our date.

Meleena likewise extended her hand, shook his then moved next to Dalencia. Their *'I told you so'* looks soon disappeared like a dog's tail between its legs.

After the brief exchange of courtesies, Didier and I walked beyond the black wrought iron gate, disappeared down the sidewalk and pass the wide trunk of an old oak tree. We arrived at the bus stop a half block away and waited for the next Downtown streetcar.

"You look huggable," I whispered.

Apparently, being with this stranger has obviously removed restraints from your thoughts and the freedom to express them. You know how bitter an unripe fruit. So, take your time. You're not getting younger, but there's no need to rush anything, my inner voice advised.

"That is a nice thing to say."

"It looks like we got here just in time," I said, pointing toward the streetcar that was a block away.

"I hope that you do not mind," he said, holding my hand like dough that needed to be kneaded.

"It's fine," I said, pretending to be unmoved but on the inside felt my resolve dissolving. I wanted to inhale him as we stood near a small group of tipsy tourists.

"There's not much traffic out tonight," I said, engaging in useless small talk that only betrayed my tongue-tied behavior.

We boarded the crowded streetcar. He stood next to me as I sat on the varnished seat. A passenger gave up his seat so that we could sit together. The windows were opened and the heavy air filled the streetcar like a thick fume. We inched closer to each other until our shoulders touched then we grinned and squirmed like hyperactive children.

"All eyes are on us, Mavielle," he whispered, sliding his arm around my shoulder like a blanket.

His and Nana's words reverberated like a jungle drum and made my smile blossom.

"And ours are on each other," I whispered, looking at him like a bride at her groom.

The Ride Home

10:35. Our roundtrip Downtown was over. We returned to a darkened library where our paths crossed hours earlier which now seemed as distant as last year.

As midnight approached, like Cinderella, the door on this evening was about to close and we'd return to our old lives.

"Are you all right, Mavielle?"

"Oh, it was just a fly," I replied, laughing, shooing away Nana's voice.

I pictured her standing with her hands on her hips, looking and laughing at us saying, *Look, Mr. Frenchman. You like her. She likes you. Go ahead, kiss, sweat and call it night! She's not getting any younger.*

"Pardon?"

"Ah, it was just an amusing thought," I said, laughing.

"Mavielle, would you like to see my flat?"

"What?!" Not sure of his intentions, I made mine quite clear, "Just so you know. We've had dinner and I'm not about to be your dessert. It's been a *looong* time since I've had to beat someone," I warned, raising my fists, imitating the Ali shuffle.

"I just want you to see where I live," he explained, looking a little terrified.

"Okay, just as long as there's no funny stuff."

"Mavielle, I pro-meeze I will do nothing to damage the openness I feel with you," he reassured, tilting his head like a child wanting to please his mother.

"I've had a blast. I enjoyed meeting you. We've had a nice time at the party. The streetcar ride was pleasant but I don't know you from Jack the Ripper," I explained.

"It is understandable that you feel that way. I do nothing to create a problem."

For all he knew, I could be what I suspected of him.

"Now that we've had this little chat, you can show me where you live."

Since this afternoon, he demonstrated that he posed no threat to me and behaved like I posed none to him.

We got into my car, which ironically was pumpkin-colored then headed towards his Uptown flat and arrived a few minutes later. Before I could turn the engine off, he jetted out, raced to the driver's side and opened my door. He could have easily pulled me into his arms, but he didn't. And I liked that he didn't.

Under the soft glow of the amber-colored street lamp, we stood on the sidewalk, talked, laughed, and kicked at the gravel like nervous teenagers. The glow from the street lamp fell on us like a theater spotlight. It felt as if we were on a stage *again* and *all* eyes of the night were on us.

"It's very quiet here."

"Yes, it is," he replied proud of his neighborhood.

After a few minutes, he invited me inside.

"How long have you lived here?" I asked, approaching the vestibule.

"One year. I will return to Lysene soon. I live a very simple life as you will see."

"Hold on," I said, turning away. I opened my purse and groped for my knife. "Okay, we can go up for a few minutes but then I'll have to leave."

He took my hand and led me up a dimly lit hardwood, spiral staircase, a common feature in old New Orleans cathouses.

He jiggled the key a few times before unlocking the deadbolt. I clutched my knife as he reached for the light switch. Once inside, the echo of our footsteps on the hardwood floors made the sweetest sound that bounced against the walls and ceiling like music.

"I don't have much furniture but it is home," he apologized.

"It doesn't matter. Sometimes less is best."

"This is the living room. I have a lovely balcony that reminds me of home," he said, touring and moving beyond the small galley before returning to the living room.

"You have a quaint home."

"This is my bedroom."

"Uh-uh," I interjected, shaking my head and refusing to cross the threshold.

A little nervous, I hurried to his colorful sofa—black and gold velvet with a fleur de lis motif. I rested one hand on the sofa's arm and the other wrapped around my knife in my purse.

"Mavielle, would you like something to drink? I have iced tea and diet cola?" he offered, sitting at the other end of the sofa as timid as I was.

"I'll have the iced tea, no ice, please. Thank you."

Hmm, no sensory deadening alcohol, that's a good sign. Good thing it's not 7-Up or he'd be in trouble. But that's information best kept between you and Nana, my inner voice observed.

We sipped our iced tea between stories about his hometown and our families. Eventually, we became more relaxed around each other. I let go of my knife, but kept it near.

"It's getting late and I really must be leaving," I said, glancing at my watch walking to the door.

He cleared his throat. But I didn't stop or turn around. He took one step towards me as I reached for the doorknob. I froze to an inaudible, "Simon said, stop." He took another step then tapped me on the shoulder. I turned slowly and noticed his wet, sad eyes.

"Mavielle. Thank you for a nice e-ve-ning. Thank you for not being afraid to come to my home. I pro-meeze I do nothing to damage that. It is the best time today I ever have. Thank you."

He made no aggressive movements as he opened the door and walked me to my car.

"I don't want you to go, but I know you must. May I have your keys, please?"

"Why? Are you going to throw them away?"

"Oh no, I open the door for you."

He held my hand like it was fine china then helped me into my car. I started the engine and inched forward. In an instant, I got distracted by the red glow of the taillights that broke the plane of the soft stream of light from the street lamp. He held and walked alongside my car like a secret service agent.

"Mavielle, may I have your telephone number?" he asked, pushing these words from his mouth, looking down and making sure I did not roll over his foot.

"246-9929."

"246-9929," he repeated, committing it to memory.

"Mavielle, I have something else to ask of you."

"What is it?"

"Would it be okay to embrace you?" he asked, his voice trembling.

I knew it. I knew it. I knew it. Voulez-vous your big toe, there it is. Sooner or later, he was going to show his spots! All of that soft, sweet talking was just a game. Play along and see what he does but be on your guard, my inner voice sounded this message of alarm.

"I am sorry," he apologized, sensing my defensiveness.

"One quick embrace."

He opened his arms like a pair of giant dove's wings, invited me in then enveloped me like a secret he was entrusted to keep.

"Thank you," he whispered, softly kissing my left cheek then the right.

Ribbons in the Sky by Stevie Wonder played on the car's radio and filled the air. My humming was bad but my singing even worse and we laughed heartily at both.

Be aware of sweet things whispered in the ear! Your next investment? An auditory enhancing device. That way, you can be exercise selective hearing by adjusting a button, my inner voice suggested.

"You like to dance?" he asked softly in my ear.

"I like."

"Perhaps we go dance some time?"

"I really must go home," I said, reluctantly wiggling from his embrace.

"Perhaps we see each other tomorrow?"

"What do you have in mind?" I asking, narrowing my eyes.

"Do you like to swim?"

"I *don't* know how to swim but my son Evan likes to swim."

"What about you? Do you have a preference?"

"Swimming is fine," I said, ignoring his follow-up questions.

"Are you sure?"

"So what's a good time for us to come?"

"10:30. Is that okay?"

"Sure. We'll be here."

"There is no need for you to bring any towels. I wait for you and Evan and also prepare dinner for us."

"You don't have to do that."

"I would like to," he said, eyes shining like new coins.

"Then we accept."

As I drove away and looked into my rearview mirror, he stood under the soft street lamp like a garden statue.

International Weekend

12:15. Drip. Drip. Drip. Like a leaky faucet, the steady rhythm of the bright red light flashed on the answering machine. Tired but exhilarated, I pressed, "Play."

"Ah, Mavielle. It's Didier. I call to say, thank you for a ve-ry pleasant e-ve-ning. I to-tal-ly enjoy you conversations. It was ve-ry nice. Bye-bye."

I did what pleased me without input from an inner voice.

"Hello. Didier. It's Mavielle," I said, hoarse from the night air.

"Oh, it is so ve-ry nice to hear you voice again. I stay awake and hope that I hear from you. Thank you ve-ry much to call me."

"I called to let you know that I arrived home safely and to confirm that I had given you a right number," I said, yawning.

We kept our first telephone conversation short. Afterwards, I fell back onto my pillow all dreamy-eyed, relived the events of yesterday then fell into a deep sleep.

The phone rang before seven.

"All right, Mavielle. Don't leave out anything. I have been waiting to call you since last night," an inquisitive Dalencia demanded.

"Hello," I answered in a groggy voice as she ignored the procession of *I'm not awake yet* yawns.

"All right, Mavielle. Don't leave anything out!"

"Good morning, Dalencia," I said, sounding hung-over.

"Don't good morning me. I want details, lots of them."

"What a strange request from someone who refused to hook me up with one of her single friends."

"That was yesterday. So tell me —"

"Tell you what?"

"You know what!" she demanded.

"Now, ain't that personal?"

"Well, it might be personal, but I need to know what happened last night."

"*Need* to know?"

"You know good and well what I want to know. Your date with the Frenchman. What did you do? Where did you go? Did he kiss you? Will you see him again? What time did you get home?" she interrogated.

"What time is it anyway?"

"It's time for you to answer my questions."

"Why don't I write a report and send it to you!"

"You don't have to be like that," she replied, irritated.

"Oh, no!" I exclaimed looking at the clock on the wall.

"What is it?"

"We'll have to talk later. I have to get out of here by 7:30."

"Well, you can go after you tell me what I want to know," she pressed. But to no avail.

"Dalencia, really, I'll call you later."

"Yeah. Right," she responded not believing me.

"I'll talk with you later," I said then hung up.

Click. Another call.

"Hello," I said, still sounding a little hoarse.

"All right, girlfriend. Let's have it. Don't leave out one drop of sweat. I wants to know about heavy breathing, spankings, and everything before, during, *and* after," the woman's voice said, sounding like she inhaled high octane coffee.

"Good morning, Nana. I hate to disappoint you, but nothing happened. In response to your 411, I have nothing delicious to report."

"I have to see this man myself and find out what's his problem."

"What problem?"

"Was there any heavy breathing?" she asked bluntly.

"Just because nothing happened, you assume he must have a problem?"

"Did he even try?"

"If only you'd had been a fly on the wall. You'd know."

"Wait till the next time you hook up with him."

"Who says I'm going to see him again?"

"The way you were looking when you left here yesterday, I knew he would try something. And if not the first time, he'd work things out until — ."

"Sorry, Nana, I have to go."

"So where are you going this early in the morning?"

"I'm headed too the weekly social gathering spot where we all have to go eventually."

"Well that ain't ladies room, so it's got to be the grocery store," she replied. "Yeah, you better go before it gets too crowded."

"I'll have to call you later," I said, cutting our conversation short.

"You can't be nice to some people," she complained, refusing to hang up.

"Nothing happened."

"You never answered my question," she reminded.

"And that would be?"

"Are you going to see him again?"

"I would like to."

My next date with Didier was a piece of personal paradise I was not ready to share with anyone except Evan.

"So what did y'all do last night? Played strip poker? Swung from the ceiling like Tarzan and Jane or walked around y'all private garden like Adam and Eve?"

"You're not even close."

"So how close did he get?"

"Not as close as you think. We walked around the library and took a streetcar ride Downtown. He went to his place. I went to mine. There *was no* heavy breathing, *no* backseat commotion, and definitely *no* jungle fever happening anywhere."

"Did he come over to your place?"

"As I mentioned before, he went to his place. I went to mine."

"Did you kiss him?"

"No. I did not kiss *him*."

But she didn't ask if he kissed me. They were quick pecks that didn't really qualify as bona fide kisses. But that was not her question.

"Did he—"

"Nana, I really need to get out of here."

"Don't forget to call me as *soooon* as you get back. Don't *haave* me waiting till Juvember. You hear me, Mavielle? I know where you live heffa," she threatened, laughing.

Your friends are sure curious about what you do. But we know nothing happened, my inner voice confirmed.

Second Date

10:45. Evan and I arrived at Didier's fifteen minutes late. When we pulled up, he was pacing back and forth on the sidewalk like an expectant father in the waiting room.

"I have been most anxious for you."

"I'm sorry. There was unusually heavy traffic."

"Mavielle, it is so strange for me to be so anxious about anyone. I *never* wait before for anyone as I do you. I do not know what is happening to me," he said with a confused look.

"We're here now," I replied, patting him on his shoulder.

"Are we still going to the pool?" Evan interjected.

"Of course. Let me get the towels and lock the door," Didier said, sprinting upstairs like his pants were on fire. He returned with a thick towel draped over his shoulder, the others stuffed into his blue backpack.

We arrived at the pool and he gave us a grand tour.

"Over here is where you dress Mavielle."

"Evan you dress here in the men's room. I will stand out here and wait for you both."

"Didier, may I have one of the towels, please?" my voice echoed from the ladies' room.

"Why? Are you not going to swim with Evan and me?"

"I told you last night that I didn't know how to swim."

"I will show you," he offered.

I removed the towel when we got closer to the pool. His eyes grew as big as half dollars then he licked his lips as if someone rang the dinner bell.

"Mavielle! You have a beautiful body! I will let nothing happen to you or Evan!" he exclaimed, his eyes searching my body like a landmark.

Didier was the first in the pool, then Evan. I sat on the edge then slid in, but held on.

"You can let go, Mavielle, I will not let you drown."

"If I drown, I'll have to hurt you."

"You should have no worry. I will hold you. I will let nothing happen to you," he said, convincing me to let go.

In the pool, Evan swam like a pro but I flapped like a fish on dry land and accidentally kicked Didier in a sensitive area. He went under then resurfaced red-faced. I didn't need a degree in common sense to know that it was time for me to get out of the water. I shivered like a newborn as Didier led me to the hot tub.

"We can sit in here until you get warm. If Evan wants to go for another swim, I will take him," he offered in a slightly altered voice.

After he and Evan swam the width of the pool a couple of times, he returned to the hot tub and noticed I was a little limp.

"Mavielle, are you okay?!"

"I'm fork-tender," I said in a weak voice, eyes barely opened.

First he wanted to drown you. Then he wanted to steam cook you. What's next? my inner voice inquired.

"Evan, we should take your mother home. I don't think she's feeling well!"

"Okay!" Evan shouted, wiping excess water from his face.

"May I have a towel, please?" I asked, regaining my senses. Didier watched with sad eyes as I concealed my body.

"Thank you," I responded, wrapping the towel loosely around my hips.

"No, thank you," he said, ogling.

We headed back to his flat for a late lunch. After Evan and I set the table, we all sat in the living room, laughed at our experiences at the pool and took pictures for our scrapbook.

"Evan. Mavielle. I hope that you like what I prepare," he said, summoning us to the table.

Our eyes grew wide as sliced andouie as we looked at New Orleans styled red beans and rice with a curious *French* twist.

"Mom, there are peanuts sprinkled on top of the beans," Evan whispered.

Red beans and rice with sausage; red beans and rice with fried fish or fried oysters, red beans and rice with pork chops or fried chicken but red beans and rice with peanuts. This is a first! an inner voice hammered.

Evan and I looked at each other amused. Didier sat across from us proud of his culinary creativity and sensed that we were a little skeptical.

"Evan. Mavielle. Eat up," he prodded.

"Mom, this is good!"

"This is *very* good," I concurred

"I was not sure that you would like it. I do not eat much meat," Didier confessed, looking a little embarrassed.

After we finished lunch and burped, we took a short leisurely walk through his neighborhood.

Depending on how the beans are cooked, it's always a good idea to be in the open air. You know how people don't like to claim those smelly oops, my inner voice kidded.

"Didier. Evan and I had a *very* nice time today. Thank you for the swim and the red beans and rice."

"And the peanuts!" Evan exclaimed.

"And the peanuts. It was delicious."

"You and Evan are welcome here anytime."

"Thank you. It's a 40 minute drive home and we really must be leaving before it gets dark."

"I wish that you and Evan could stay."

"It would be nice, but we have to go."

"Wait, I walk you to you car."

"I liked the pool," Evan commented.

"I like that you and your mother spend time with me in my home. Thank you. Perhaps we see each other again?"

"For sure," I responded, winking at him.

"Tomorrow?" Evan inquired, looking at me for a 'yes.'

"We'll see." I replied, rubbing Evan's cheek.

Like the night before, Didier stood on the sidewalk with a long face and continued to wave until we were almost out of sight.

"I call you!" he yelled before we disappeared.

Evan and I arrived home 45 minutes later. We showered and fell quickly asleep.

Didier's voice filled my room as I slept. I awoke the next morning and listened to the message he left during the night.

"Ah, Mavielle. I was dreaming about you and you beautiful body. I am most anxious to see you."

I saved that message as a pick-me-up.

Planting Memories

Lake Pontchartrain near the Seabrook Bridge.

As we sat on a bench facing the Lake, Didier reminded me of heartbreaking news.

"In a few days, I will return to Lysene."

"What?!" I exclaimed, eyes blinking uncontrollably.

"Please, let me explain. If we have meet before my transfer, I would not be leaving," he said, lifting my hand and tossing it between his like a hot potato.

"I'm shocked and sad that you're leaving. But I also understand what it's like to be homesick. I moved away from my family and felt lost even though I met new people."

"I do miss my home. It has been difficult for me. I have problems to adjust to culture here and in France. It is very different. Also my English is no too good," he said, supporting his reason for leaving.

"I miss you and you haven't left yet."

"I miss you every time I leave you and Evan,'" he replied with an agonized look.

"How many days before you leave? Never mind, we have some living to do."

We did not wallow in the sadness of his pending departure. We had memories to plant. Determined to make the best of the time we had, we browsed the "Living" section of the *Picayune*.

"I admit I was afraid of you in the beginning. Then after we talked, I become comfortable around you."

"So if you were afraid, why did you come to the party? I didn't know where you lived?" I inquired, hunching my shoulders.

"I wanted to. I enjoyed you poetries and feel that you were a nice person. I watched you with Evan. You do not hit him or scream or fuss at him. I *love* the way you love him."

"Thank you. Evan makes it easy to love him. And I'm not saying that because I'm his mother."

"I wish that I know that kind of love."

"I did."

"I know that if we have a child together you will love him as you do Evan."

"Hold your horses. I'm done with diapers and breast-feeding," I said, looking at him under-eyed.

"I was just thinking about the future. That is all."

"So was I!" I said, raising one brow.

"Mavielle, I tell you that I am very proud to be with you?"

"All the time."

"I like the way I laugh when I am with."

"I give you what I get from you."

"What?"

"You give me a reason to be open-hearted and free again."

"Thank you," he said, rocking me in his arms from side to side.

The first place on our list was the Greek Festival. We walked across the Marconi Street Bridge, entered the festival gate and encountered as many stares as we did at the party. After sampling the food, we moved on.

"What we do next?" he asked like a child at his first carnival.

"A movie?" I suggested.

"Mavielle, please do not be sad," he said, brushing my check with his hand, arousing a temporary smile.

"If you hadn't touched me in here," I said, putting his hand over my heart, "then I wouldn't be sad at all."

We arrived at the foot of Canal Street where there was a hub of activities. We walked down Decatur to Café du Monde and ate beignets, then stepped next door and sampled creamy pralines from Aunt Sally's Praline Shoppe. We passed a patio restaurant where the music of a jazz band competed with riverboat whistles and the sound of waves being pushed by huge ships guided from behind by tugboats. We roamed through the French Market, zigzagged from Esplanade to N. Rampart to St. Phillip and ended up at Croissant D'Or where we shared a slice of fresh strawberry cake.

After the Italian movie, we were lured by live music and echoes of laughter from Woldenberg Park. We joined the crowd by the river and danced as if we had all the time in the world. Like tourists, we posed in front of the riverboat Natchez and noticed a plume of black smoke from a docking ferryboat then gravitated towards it.

No Regrets

Capt. Stumpf Ferry. Bottom deck. Didier and I stared at the propellers as they whipped the water like egg whites at high speed in a mixing bowl. Hungry seagulls hovered and screamed at generous passengers until they tossed morsels of stale bread into the air like Mardi Gras beads.

"Mavielle, he whispered in my ear. "You are precious. You should always be treated like a queen."

"Well, King Didier," I said, smiling which cheek to cheek and stroking the back of his head. "This is the first time in my life that I've known this kind of tenderness. And I'm glad it was you who opened this door."

"I do not write poetries. I have been searching for the words to explain how it feels when I am with you. I only find the words to explain what it is like without you."

"You don't have to be a poet to say what is in your heart," I said, rubbing his chest.

Not another word passed between us and we continued to embrace as the ferry docked.

We picked Evan up from his school then headed to City Park along the scenic route of Bayou St. John.

We parked near the lagoon and came across a gang of crumb-snatching squirrels that scattered as Evan raced towards the merry-go-round. Enticed by his laughter, we joined him and spun around and around heads tilted back, eyes closed and giggled like untroubled children. In the warmth of the afternoon sunlight and full to overflowing with wonder, we staggered to a nearby bench until the world stopped spinning.

"I pro-meeze to take Evan to eat pizza before I leave," Didier mumbled as we stood now able to walk in a straight line.

Evan swung back and forth from our bent elbows the way he did from a low-hanging branch as we walked to the car.

We drove Uptown to a cozy pizzeria frequented by college students. The waiter seated us at a table in the middle of the outdoor patio. As if someone yelled "Cut" on a movie set, an eerie hush replaced all activity from busboys clanging dishes to drumming footsteps of hustling waiters to a pot of simmering conversations. We ignored them all.

"I know it will be difficult for us tomorrow. I will miss you and Evan ve-ry much. I hope that you will accept the gifts I buy for you."

"You didn't have to do that."

"Hue Hoo!" Evan exclaimed at the thought of getting a present.

"Evan!" I gently scolded.

"It is all right, Mavielle," he said, eyes beaming tenderly at Evan.

"If it is okay with you, I would like to give them to you and Evan this evening?"

"Can we mom, please, pretty please?"

"Okay."

After dinner, we went back to his flat.

"I want to thank you and Evan for being so nice to me while I am here in the United States," he said, handing us neatly wrapped gifts. "I ask that you open them after I leave," he requested. We obliged.

After we took pictures, huddled in the middle of his living room and cried a community of tears. It felt like a funeral and all that was missing, was a body.

Au Revoir

7:55. As I drove to Didier's, I cried as hard as I pushed in childbirth. Before turning the corner, I brushed away the tears with the back of my hand that flowed like a river then rubbed lotion to erase their white tracks from my face.

We stood on the sidewalk as we did many times before but this time was different. His bags and other remnants of his life in the United States were stacked in the vestibule.

"Bonjour, Didier," I greeted with a manufactured smile.

"Bonjour, mon chère."

"Merci beaucoup, monsieur. I tried to hold back my tears but I couldn't. I don't *want* to be brave. I *want* you to know that you're inside of these tears," I said, eyes still swollen from crying.

He folded his arms around me, rocked me like a baby and gently stroked my hair.

"Ah Mavielle," he whispered. "I pro-meez to call you when I arrive in Lysene. I pro-meez to write often. I pro-meez that we will see each other again. I pro-meez never to forget how we crossed into each other's worlds and opened a door that only time will close. I pro-meez to never forget you or Evan and how you love him," he whispered in my ear. "It hurts me to leave. I wish that we meet before I give a request to return to Lysene," he explained, crying.

"I want you to know that you are taking my heart with you over the ocean," I said, weeping.

We held each other as if it had to last forever.

"Please do not cry," he pleaded, leaning my head tenderly against his shoulder. "I lick you tears and take them with me as souvenirs."

That was profound. He licked your tears, my inner voice offered as testimony to his sensitivity and humanity.

His friend, Bolarz arrived moments later to drive him to the airport.

In the rearview mirror, I looked behind; he looked ahead. We disappeared from each other's sights but not each other's memories.

The stranger in the khaki shorts, black-ribbed socks, brown shoes with black shoelaces, green-rimmed glasses etched his place in my heart forever.

Later that evening when I returned home, I unwrapped one of the presents. It was a book of poetry in which he inscribed:

"Chère Mavielle,

Merci mille fois pour tes merveilleuses poésies et les moments que nous avons passée ensemble.

À bientôt,

Didier"

Dear Mavielle,

Thanks a million for your marvelous poetry and the moments that we have passed together.

See you soon,

Didier.

Moving On

A bubble bath by candelight, Brook Benton on the stereo, and one glass of Zinfandel. It doesn't get any better than this. And you need to treat yourself more often. Now, don't this feel good? my inner voice encouraged.

The phone rang.

"Mmm, hello," I whispered in a faraway voice.

"Mavielle?" the soft voice responded.

"Mmm, hello," I repeated like a broken record.

"Bonjour, Mavielle. It is Didier!"

"Ahh, Didier. Comment ça va?!"

"Bien but perhaps not as well as you," he responded, sensing my mood.

"It is better now that I hear your voice!"

"Mavielle, are you alright?" he inquired not sure what to make of my behavior.

"Oui, Monsieur, pour quoi?"

"Are you sure that you are all right?"

"I'm enjoying a wonderful bubble bath by candlelight, un verre de vin, soft music and missing you terribly."

"I wish that I never leave," he admitted. "I keep my pro-meez to you to call when I arrive in Lysene."

"Thank you. So how was your flight?"

"It was long and lonesome. I think of you and Evan all the way and feel very sad that I leave you."

"It's been hard on this end also."

"I keep my word to call and I will also keep my word to write often."

"I appreciate that. I know that this is an international call and—."

"It is no problème. I need to hear you voice. How is Evan? I tell my family about the two of you. My sister, Michelle would like very much to meet you and Evan. I show to her and my nieces the pictures that I take of you and Evan."

"Ahh, that's so sweet. Before I forget, thank you for the book of poetry. Evan likes his presents also. He's asleep and will be sorry that he didn't get to talk with you."

"I will call back and talk to him. I call also to ask to you if you would like to visit Lysene and hope that you will like it here. The people are very friendly. It is near the Alps. There is much open space. It is very quiet. I take you to see where I went to school. We can tour the city and visit the small shops."

"It sounds lovely."

"I buy a ticket for you."

"I would love to visit Lysene and to meet your family but school has just started and it is not a good time to leave Evan," I said, floating from side to side in the tub.

"I understand."

"Perhaps another time," I said optimistically.

"I miss you and Evan very much. I will write to you tomorrow," he said sadly.

"And I will write you also. Au revoir."

"À bientôt not au revoir, Mavielle. I will be here in Lysene for two weeks then I go to Rome to teach and to continue my studies. I will call you when I get to Rome."

Didier kept all of his promises. An international relationship would not work and we could no longer ignore this sad reality.

It hurts now but allow yourself time to heal. And as you glance through the best time of your life like yesterday's newspaper, just remember that you've experienced something some people never do in a lifetime. Keep these memories alive. Whenever you feel lonely, go to a quiet place and recall how a colorfully dressed stranger in khaki shorts, black-ribbed socks, brown shoes with black shoelaces, green-rimmed glasses changed your life. Now it's time to reconnect with your world, my inner voice counseled.

Life, Love and Friends

Four months later. I was ready to emerge from this cocoon and fly. In need of a little boost, I reached out to my friend.

"Hi, Nana. Can I come over?"

"Come on."

I pulled into her driveway. Nana stood behind her glass storm door like a mother waiting all day for her child to march up the sidewalk from school.

"Well, well, well. Look what the cat brung to my front door. Girl, Mavielle, you look like—"

"Death warmed over?"

"No, baby," she said softly. "I was going to say, you look like you could use a friend."

"I can," I said, lowering my head.

"Girrl, I thought you dropped off the face of the earth. I was just kidding about Fed-Ex'ing your butt to the moon. You said you would call me back, but you didn't. So I figured *she'll call when she's good and ready.* So you must be ready."

"I had a few things to work out. That's all," I mumbled, walking behind her like follow-the-leader.

"You should know that you can count on me. I give you a hard time sometimes, but you're my sister," she said, curling her lips at the corner and hugging me with her eyes.

As she locked the door, I planted myself on the sofa beneath the same gold-framed mirror where she performed a make-over.

"You know, I'm dying to get the low down about your date with his MacGyver looking self. But, I also know when you're ready, you'll talk."

"Thanks. I appreciate your understanding."

"No problem. So are you here to talk?" she asked, stretching her eyes.

"No. Not yet."

"How about some Devalicious coffee?" she asked, tucking her hands under her thighs.

"Sure, why not?"

"You're in my living room not a funeral home. You may feel a little dead inside, but you're very alive and still among the living. I got something that'll pick you up. There ain't nothing like music to get you out of a funk along with a cup of Devalicious," she analyzed, turning on the stereo and queuing *I'm Every Woman* by Chaka Khan.

"Turn it up," I requested, needing to feel the music move through me.

"Girl, I went to this funeral the other day," she said, smacking her lips. "And this old woman walked up to me and started telling me all kinds of stuff. That old ta-ta had me rolling till I almost peed on myself."

"I could use a good laugh. What did she say?"

"She said she buried *two* husbands because they couldn't handle her sex drive. Mavielle, the woman was 95!"

"95?"

"You heard me!" she said, stretching her eyes. "95! And the last husband died 5 years ago. That means she was 90 years old still getting her freak on. Now she's 'Every Woman' and I dare not picture her in a teddy," she gasped. "And then, when I was in the kitchen helping to serve the family, this old man comes in and gets *all* up in my face 'cause he didn't have a fork to eat with."

"And you said something colorful like —"

"I told him, 'well if you bend over and dig hard enough, I'm sure you'll find one and pull it out of your butt!'"

I laughed so hard I felt alive again.

"That'll teach folks to mess with me when I'm doing my best to help somebody," she said, strutting boastfully.

I took several sips of her special brew and felt very relaxed. Droopy-eyed and nearly semi-conscious, I giggled at any and everything. As the aroma of coffee and chicory and something else filled her house and our cups *many* times, she related an experience about a special brew.

"Girl, I'm used to having my Devalicious coffee no matter where I am. One morning I had just finished brewing a pot, spiked it with 80 proof, dark rum then here comes this big shot executive who drank all of my doggone coffee! And I called him every name under the sun and then some — to his face," she said pressing her lips together.

"What did he do?"

"That *man* had the nerve to laugh. But he apologized then staggered to the conference room but not before he gave me $100 to replace what he drank."

"That must have been one powerful pot of coffee!" I said, bobbing my head like a yo-yo.

"I know it don't feel like it now, but it'll be all right," she said, pouring a fifth cup then putting the pot on the silver tray on her mahogany coffee table.

After a moment of silence, we laughed then sat back as if to resume a game of poker to call each other's bluffs.

"*Mmm*, this is good *soo*, I mean, *soo* good," I said, shaking my head to reshuffle words hung up somewhere between my brain and tongue.

"I knooow," she agreed, stretching her lips.

"What brand is this again, I mean, flavor, no brand," I said, confused as when I had a concussion.

"Lu-zzzi-ane. New Orleans Blend."

"SSSomething's different about the taste."

"I told you it was ssspecial."

"And wwwhat makes it soo special?"

"Amaretta. Ama—Amaretto."

"Nana, you know I-I-I don't drink!"

"Girl, this, this coffee will keep you from jumping around like uh, like uh, like a bunny rabbit on a cheap high." she said reconnecting her thoughts and laughing.

"Are you trying to get me drrrunk?"

"Me?" she asked, hiccupping and pointing at me.

"Yesss, you," I said, dropping my head like it was too heavy on my shoulders.

"Not me. You're the one drinking. I'm just trying to help you close a door."

"You're slick. Well, here's to Deva for being my sssister and friend."

"Yes, I am and here's to opening doors and closing our legs!"

"Yes, you are and here's to l-l-life, l-l-love and the pursuit of anything that needs to be pursued!"

"You better know and here's to friends who help friends when *Love Don't Live Here Any More*," she sang, loosely. "Okay, that's enough of this BS. You ready to talk now?" she said, changing gears with no hint of slurring.

"I thought you said I could talk when *I'm* ready?"

"And you believe *me*? And I thought you knew *me*," she replied, crossing her eyes.

"No, I thought you knew *me*," I said, leaning forward, staring in both pairs of her eyes.

"I do!" she proclaimed boldly.

"Because if you did, you would know that alcohol does *not* loosen my lipss. It only makes me sleep without counting them sheep," I yawned then fell asleep.

"Mavielle! Mavielle! I don't believe you. I bet if I get a hat pin and stick your skinny butt, you'll wake up then!"

Like a satisfied kitty, I stretched, purred then snored.

"I know you better wake your tired butt up and talk to me," she said, fussing and laughing then realized she was talking to herself.

Barely touching me with her finger, I fell over like a drunken domino. After she staggered to the closet, got a sheet and covered me like a deceased patient on a hospital gurney, then plopped down in her chair.

"Rest my friend 'cause when you wake up, I wants to hear everything!"

Two hours later, I awoke and noticed a hat pin on the coffee table with only a vague recollection of it.

Nana, slouched in her chair, head bowed and hands folded as if she fell asleep while praying, snored like a chainsaw. Her empty cup was on the floor next to the front leg of her chair like *it* had passed out.

I covered her with a sheet, glanced at the hat pin, laughed then thought appreciatively, *my friend, my sister, now that's Lagniappe.*

reflecting

a place to reflect

Autumn of Life

Our Father, thank you for
The singular beauty
Of a harvest moon as it
Breaks the horizon and
Touches us with its peacefulness;
Thank you for
The hollowness of green leaves
Dismantled in October on their hiatus
From summer's heat which
Explode in a riot of autumn colors then
Dress to match changing temperatures.

Thank you for

The cycle of life that

Awakens in us a flame as ancient

As polished stones in a

Natural history that

Sweeps across the landscape to an intersection

Where time and season

Meet, where leaves

Judged by their color

Disappear like chameleons

Changing with their backgrounds.

Thank you for

Young trees that

Slip into deep sleep and

In their own rhythm of

Sleeping and waking, they

Stand like thin fingers that

Give in to winter and stiffen

In a noiseless hush,

Like a kite on the wind.

Thank you for

Falling leaves that speak in low voices that

Even in perfect silence

Their sound is invisible

Until like shriveled aborted flowers

They crunch

Under heavy footsteps.

Thank you for the music of
Strong winds that
Sounds like hard laughter
Running through the forest
Scattering seeds of life.

Thank you Jah for
The singular beauty of
Autumn leaves that
Drop like
Parachutes
And fall like
Tears until
They cover earth below;
From lifeless
In winter
To fertile
In spring
As testimony to You.
We thank you,
Our Father,
Our King.

Blessings

In the bosom of night
I feel the pulse of the minute hand
Punch through the wall and
Beat in sync with my heart.
I cried tears I thought were my own and
Became aware that similar tears with
Different purposes
Had fallen down the cheeks
Of generations before me.
In the bosom of night's calm
I thank Jah; that He
Sits on high and
Looks down low; that He
Remembers our morning footprints
In afternoon sand
Long after they
Get erased
By incoming tides; that He
Knows the names and elements of galaxies
Beyond our reach; that He
Authorizes the sun's graceful exit
From evening's stage; that He
Gives power to the moon to
Rise in its slow muted rhythm; that He
Pushes aside clouds that hide
Night's irreplaceable jewelry; that He

Makes the pine trees of Forest Hill

Dance in their fragrances; that He

Allows constant winds to

Bend trees

Strong and upright along

Forgotten plantation roads; that He

Knows the history of

Muffled tears behind our eyes; that He

Hears unpretentious prayers

Before they leave our lips; that He

Answers them all,

Sometimes, 'Yes'

Sometimes, 'No; that He

Satisfies our hunger for mercy;

Quenches our thirst for justice; that He

Knows that absent a relationship with Him

We are like fish out of the water

That flip-flop on dry land; that He

Keeps open the door

We keep closing; that He

Knows how much we can bear; that He

Eases pain that throbs

Loud as waterfalls; that He

Takes note of weeping willows

Planted by the water and that

Lean over from the banks

As if praising Him; that He

Ordains when clouds of new butterflies should

Fill a lavender sky; that He

Hears and understands whispers of the ocean; that He

Hears the cries of cornstalks; that He

Knows how many honey-colored

Strands are in the tassels of corn; that He

Takes note of the tireless footsteps of ants; that He

Knows how many times per second a pair of

Hummingbird's wings flap; that He

Reads the heart of the dying in the very moment

That breath leaves their bodies; that He

Keeps in His memory

Our loved ones as they

Enter deep, restful sleep; that He

Soothes us when their absences

Are too heavy to carry.

Yes, in the bosom of night

Let us be thankful that it is Jah who

Sits on high and

Looks down low and that His

Thoughts are higher than ours.

Early morning

During the wee hours of morning
When the amount of light
Is bent by a crescent moon,
When the deep hum of an electric wire
Continues after all movement has stopped,
It feels like a wave of peace has
Rolled over the land
And all friction has fallen like dominoes.
During the wee hours of morning
I yearn
For the place of my birth

Where great-uncles
Were as old as Buildings;
Where people
Rose with the sun;
Where there was life
In the colorful
Unvarnished words
Like 'hayamamdem?'
'Uhm fixin' ta
Make gro'ries,
You want
Sum'in' from the sto'?
Cookin' earl'
Or mynass?'

And songs that built life with
Memories of survival.
During the wee hours of morning
My face is among those
Creased with grief and with those who
Cling to hope as we
Mourn a city
Littered with
Rusty highway
Signs, and
Unboarded
Windows
Tilted skyward;
Abandoned

Post-Hurricane Katrina - Photograph by George W. White Jr.

Stoops where revelers
Sat and watched the
Mardi Gras Indians
Strut in their festive colors along Orleans Avenue
Towards the North Claiborne underpass;
Where jazz funerals
Moved in a solemn procession
Lead by men in top hats and tuxedos
Followed by trombone, trumpet and tambourine
En route to the cemetery,
A city of the dead within a city of the dying.
The place of my birth is now filled with
Crumbled neighborhoods with cracked,
Weed-sprouting sidewalks where century old houses got

Shoved off their foundations; they

Lean on their sides as empty

As abandoned wombs.

As life in the place of my birth

Slowly drains away,

You can hear screams

From the ruins that were ruined.

The place of my birth

Is raw with memories of a vanished past

So People get ready, there's train a comin'

'Cause progress is slow to

Restore a dislocated culture and a devastated people.

Many were hopeful to return to

Recreate the landscape

Of a former life;

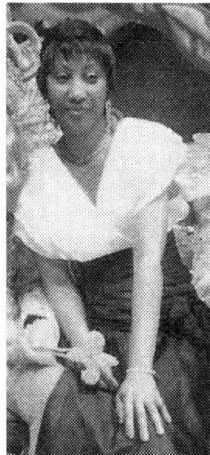

This is the place of

My birth in name only.

During the wee hours of morning

I recall my grandfather's words,

If you can't go nowhere else,

You can always go home.

As was tradition, he kept an ax in his attic

During 'storm season' - just in case

Flood waters from the Gulf,

The Mississippi and bayous came together

In a convention to swallow the land and

Everything on it, and unearth buried lies.

That time came in September 1965.

My grandfather and aunt

Climbed into their attic

As the Eye of the Storm

Passed calmly overhead, then afterwards

Furious winds unleashed its wrath and

Whipped the land into submission.

He broke through the roof

Then waited for help

An uncle rescued them in his small boat.

I was only 9 when we evacuated and abandoned

A life to which we would never return,

Except to visit

Those who did and

To bury those who would not.

Betsy swept our houses from the earth but left

A persimmon tree firmly rooted in the backyard.

We rode 82 miles to town to escape her fury and

Huddled with family on Elmira Street in Algiers

As ferocious winds screamed and as curtains of rain fell.

That time came again in August 2005,

My granddaughter was only 9.

Within the bosom of 40 years, we are bonded

In a mutual understanding

Of despair, devastation and depopulation.

I recall my grandfather's words,

If you can't go nowhere else,

You can always go home.

In the wee hours of morning,

I yearn

To visit the place of my birth

But most of it is no longer there;

The people have been scattered like seeds;

Some

Have planted themselves elsewhere;

Others

Have returned to what was left and

Endure a tsunami of bureaucratic chaos, frightening crime

And backdoor schemes that redirect funds from the have-nots

To those who have it all and who want more.

Graves of family members

Were opened;

Their remains —

Remain lost.

Lines have been redrawn to

Accommodate earthen

Levees that now swallow the land and

Obscure property lines and left-over

Memories of home.

During the wee hours of morning

As for the cycle of frustration and the profiteers of despair,

I am encouraged as "they too shall pass"

And my grandfather's word,

When you can't go nowhere else,

You can always go home

Won't haunt me anymore.

So where do we go

When home is gone?

Home is where the heart is

We can build a house

Anywhere.

St. Ann @ N. Broad Streets, New Orleans, Louisiana - Photo by Keith Medley

www.ingramcontent.com/pod-product-compliance
Lightning Source LLC
Chambersburg PA
CBHW032103080426
42733CB00006B/393